The Old Testament for Modern Readers

Also by D. B. J. Campbell

The Synoptic Gospels (John Murray)

The Old Testament for Modern Readers

D. B. J. CAMPBELL

JOHN KNOX PRESS
Atlanta, Georgia

Preface

There is no 'instant' way of understanding the Bible: it is possibly the most misunderstood of all literature. In the past, understanding of it has been limited to a few. Reverence for it has sometimes been shown in strange and even superstitious ways. Consequently many people today reject the Bible as spiritually outdated and academically unsound.

This book is designed to help the modern reader who is prepared to study the Bible objectively and persistently, especially anyone beginning a course on the Old Testament for a university qualifying examination. Cross reference and occasional recapitulation make it possible for a reader to begin at almost any point. The Revised Standard Version is used for quotations and references.

Library of Congress Cataloging in Publication Data
Campbell, D. B. J.
The Old Testament for modern readers
1. Bible. O.T.—Study—Text-books
2. Cultus, Jewish. I. Title.
BS1194.C35   1974   221.6   73–16913
ISBN 0–8042–0197–8

© D. B. J. Campbell 1972
British edition published by John Murray, London, 1972
American edition published by John Knox Press, Atlanta, Georgia, 1974

75-68606   Printed in Great Britain

Contents

1. THE OLD TESTAMENT   1

    Why the name?   1

    Is it true?   1

    The Old Testament picture   3

2. HEBREW HISTORY   5

    The outlook of Hebrew historians and writers   5

    The Deuteronomic Reform   7

    The Deuteronomic editors   8

    The construction of Hebrew history   11

3. HEBREW BELIEF IN GOD   15

    The way in which he is written about   15

    The first thousand years of Hebrew history   18

        (a) The Patriarchs   19

        (b) The wanderings in the wilderness   20

        (c) The conquest and settlement of Canaan   20

    The monarchy – from Saul to the Exile   22

    The Exile   23

    After the Exile   24

    The name of God   25

4. THE COVENANT   28

    Its inauguration   28

CONTENTS

The Covenant People 29

The Ten Commandments 30

The Book of the Covenant 34

The Ark of the Covenant 35

The prophets and the Covenant 36

5. THE MONARCHY 39

The tribal system 39

The establishment of the monarchy 42

The ideal of kingship 44

The Ideal King 46

6. THE BOOKS OF THE OLD TESTAMENT 49

Arrangement 49

The Law 50

The Prophets 50

The Writings 52

The Apocrypha 53

Wisdom Literature 54

Apocalyptic Writing 58

7. STORIES WITH SPECIAL MEANINGS 61

Who made the world? 62

Why is there sin and suffering? 63

Why different languages? 65

Why are there natural disasters? 67

Ruth 68

Jonah 69

Esther 70

Job 72

8. MIRACLES IN THE OLD TESTAMENT   75
   National   75
   Personal   78
   Topographical   79

9. PRIMITIVE RELIGIOUS BELIEFS   81
   Animism   81
   Sacred trees   82
   Sacred waters   83
   Sacred mountains and rocks   85
   Human sacrifice   88
   Holiness   89
   Baal worship and high places   92

10. THE AFTER-LIFE   96
    Official Hebrew belief   97
    Hebrew belief in general   97
    Pre-exilic belief   97
    Post-exilic belief   100

11. HEBREW FESTIVALS   104
    The Passover and Unleavened Bread   104
    Pentecost   107
    Tabernacles   108
    The Day of Atonement   110
    New Year's Day   112
    Feast of the Dedication   113
    Feast of Purim   114
    The Sabbath   114

CONTENTS

12. ISRAEL'S WORSHIP   118

    The Tabernacle   118

    Solomon's Temple   119

    Zerubbabel's Temple   119

    Herod's Temple   121

13. SACRIFICE   123

    The burnt offering   126

    The sin offering and the guilt offering   126

    The peace offering   126

    The meal offering   127

14. THE PRIESTHOOD   128

    Before the Exile   128

    During the Exile   131

    After the Exile   132

    Index   134

1. The Old Testament

Why the name?

Popular association of the word 'testament' with the making of wills very much obscures the Bible use of the word, which is derived from two sayings of St. Paul in the Second Epistle to the Corinthians. In one he speaks of himself and his fellow workers as 'ministers of a new covenant' (2 Corinthians 3 [6]). In the other he describes Jewish reading of the books of Moses as 'when they read the old covenant' (2 Corinthians 3 [14]).

The Greek word for covenant got translated into Latin sometimes as *instrumentum* and sometimes as *testamentum*, but *testamentum* prevailed and became the accepted name for the two well-known sections of the Bible. Thus, when Erasmus in 1516 edited the first printed edition of the Greek New Testament he called it *Novum Instrumentum*, but in the third edition altered it to *Novum Testamentum* (see p. 29). The title page in the Revised Standard Version has 'The New Covenant commonly called the New Testament'.

The Covenant with which the Old Testament is concerned is that which the Hebrew people believed that God had entered into with them on Mount Sinai (see p. 28). This was the beginning of their nationhood, and the background of all their thinking. It was the rallying-point of their prophets. The fidelity with which the contract was kept on the human side decided the degree of favour that might be expected from God. If it were broken irretrievably, as some prophets, notably Jeremiah, feared that it might be, a new covenant would be needed (Jeremiah 31 [31-34]).

This, the Christian Church believes, was provided by Jesus, who by his death brought about a new relationship between man and God, and who said at the Last Supper, 'This is my blood of the new covenant' (Mark 14 [24]). As the Old Testament is the record of the setting up and working out of the Old Covenant, so the New Testament is the record of the setting up and beginning of the New Covenant.

Is it true?

This is the question most frequently asked, both of the Bible as a whole, and of the Old Testament in particular. The question is closely followed by such questions as: Who wrote it? Why was it written? Were things written down at the time? How do we know what was originally written? How do we know that it was not written by impostors? Do we have to believe every word of it?

Much more useful as a starting question is: What is it?

The Old Testament is a library of thirty-nine books. The name Bible comes to us through Latin from the Greek word *biblos* (or *bublos*). The ancients used the *biblos*, the inner bark of the papyrus reed, as writing material. So, as from the reed we derive the word paper, so from the inner bark comes the word Bible.

The word Bible means a collection of books. The books are some of the histories and literature of the Hebrew people. This particular selection of books, known as the Old Testament, was not fixed by the Jews until the Council of Rabbis held about A.D. 100 at Jamnia, thirty miles west of Jerusalem. The books cover at least a thousand years.

The Old Testament might be compared with all that has been written in English over the last 1500 years. Would it be sensible to ask of the whole of English literature, including histories: Is it true? When was it written? A people is made up of individuals, some of whom write; and they write at different periods and for differing reasons. One might as well try to prove that Piers Plowman really existed, or that *The Pilgrim's Progress* is historical fact, just because the books themselves are part of English literature.

Nor is the value of our literature any the less because the stories told about King Arthur or Robin Hood are not all factual. Historians, it is true, are concerned to get facts and dates as accurate as possible. Specialists in English literature are interested in Shakespeare's sources, and whether he or Bacon wrote the plays. If they are also historians, they may think that Holinshed gave Shakespeare a distorted view of the Wars of the Roses. But such doubts in no way diminish either Shakespeare's work or English literature as a whole.

The same commonsense and use of reason must be applied to the Old Testament. This is no easy matter. There is no quick way of getting 'instant understanding' without effort. Each book, or even part of it, in the Old Testament library has to be studied carefully. The student has to ask: When was it written? Who was the author? What was his purpose? What was his form of literary expression – autobiography, biography, poetry, parable, allegory, historical narrative, historical novel? Was the author writing about something or someone of his own day, or about the past?

But, the history and literature of the Old Testament, unlike English history and literature, shows a unique unity of purpose. Although countless writers and editors over the centuries contributed to the Old Test-

2

ament, all had the same conviction that God had a special purpose for their people. This purpose is seen in all the writings, whatever their character. The divine and the human are closely woven together. It is possible to separate them, but their combined value is then destroyed.

So when we ask whether the Old Testament is true, the answer depends upon the sort of truth for which we are looking. Truth exists not merely in actual incident. The Bible has much of this sort of truth, but also much poetical truth, allegorical truth, prophetic truth, truth about human nature. It is always the underlying spiritual truth that is the more important. Some very primitive ideas of God appear in the Old Testament. They are not true from a Christian standpoint, but they were true to the people of the time.

When people ask whether they must believe every word of the Old Testament, they often mean, must they believe in it as being historically true to fact. Since only some of the books are historical, it would be absurd to believe every word in this way. And sometimes they mean, is every word to be taken as revealing God's will to man. But such a literal belief would not be very helpful, since much of the Old Testament is not at all vital to faith. Some of it is quite sordid. Insistence upon the historical truth of every word does not increase respect for the Old Testament. On the contrary it tends to degrade the Old Testament to the level of a magical book.

The modern reader of the Old Testament may well believe that the Hebrews, led by Moses, escaped from Egypt, and that God both intended and enabled them to do so; but he will not necessarily believe in the accuracy of every detail of the biblical accounts. He will believe that the Hebrews captured the city of Jericho, and will realize that, although it may have seemed right to them to suppose that God wanted the complete destruction of the city and its inhabitants, he need not follow them in this belief, nor need he believe in all the details of the operation. In some such way as this a modern reader will study and assess the material put before him.

The Old Testament picture

Old Testament history as it now reads is rather like a coloured picture – a *highly* coloured picture, and one much touched up. It is the task of the student to try to recognize the individual colours that go to make up the final picture, and the various hands that have applied them.

Alternatively, comparison may be made with the process of colour printing, in which one colour is printed at a time, yellow, blue, and red, so producing the final picture. For this particular comparison we begin with a black and white picture: this is the outline of actual

3

historical events, which can be substantially corroborated by archaeology and other material evidence. When people ask 'Is the Bible true?' they usually mean historically true and reliable. The answer is 'Yes', in so far as this outline is concerned; but it is not the final picture.

To the historical outline needs to be added the *yellow* of national pride and exaggeration, as the stories were first handed down from one generation to another. Almost invariably a nation tends to exaggerate the odds against it when celebrating victory or explaining defeat. Heroic deeds become yet more glorious with the passing of time.

So, especially glowing are the accounts of the Exodus. Did the Pharaoh himself, and all the chariots of Egypt, really pursue a few run-away slaves? Probably not, but it sounds good. The last plague, which caused a death in every Egyptian household, becomes more dramatic when described as the death of the firstborn in every family. Highly dramatized, too, is the crossing of the Red Sea, and the first great victory in Palestine, the capture of Jericho.

Folklore surrounds a figure such as Samson in much the same way as it surrounds King Arthur or Robin Hood. Popular imagination runs riot. Samson was the Hebrew Hercules, and personified the spirit of Hebrew resistance in the face of the Philistines. Through his deeds of daring the people themselves were hitting at the enemy. All these influences have to be taken into consideration when looking at Hebrew history.

The religious outlook of the writers contributed another colour to the picture – *blue* (see p. 5). They all had a strong conviction that the historical course of events had not just happened that way, but was part of God's plan. Every incident, whether of victory or defeat, was given a religious explanation, though sometimes a very crude one by New Testament standards.

Some of the Old Testament editors were priests rewriting their history during the Exile. Their interest was mainly religious, and much concerned with ritual and ceremonial, with the observance of festivals, the Sabbath, circumcision, and other religious matters. The description of the Passover ritual in Exodus 12 was written by priests for whom the festival had acquired a developed ceremonial over the centuries. In the same spirit they wrote the detailed descriptions of the Tabernacle and its furnishings, and the consecration of priests (Exodus 25-31).

Finally, *red* completes the coloured picture. This is the special religious point of view of the Deuteronomic editors. These compilers of history were profoundly influenced by the ideals set forth in the law book found in the Temple in 621 B.C., probably the book now known as Deuteronomy. They judged all actions in Hebrew history in the light of this discovery; and it is easy to detect their disapproval of all worship other than that offered at the Temple.

2. Hebrew History

The outlook of Hebrew historians and writers

The Hebrew historians, together with all other Old Testament authors, looking back on their nation's history as time went by, were firmly convinced that things did not just happen. The course of events, from the Exodus onwards, seemed to them to have an underlying purpose, and this purpose they believed to be divine. This outlook was shared by many – and who is to say that the outlook was mistaken? Christians, at least, agree that God had a plan for Israel, which was to reach its climax in the coming of Christ, a sort of final act in a divine drama.

By way of contrast, British historians looking back upon the Norman Conquest, for example, do not see it as a deliberate achievement of God. They do not maintain that the British habitation of these islands was something specially intended by God, It may well be that it *was*; but it is not usual to regard events in this way. The Hebrew historians, on the other hand, saw history from just such a distinctive outlook.

Hebrew events can be looked upon as ordinary history. The Hebrews were a race of people of nomadic origin who, after a period of slavery in Egypt, invaded, and eventually settled down in, the land of Canaan. They developed a monarchy, had a civil war, and suffered domination from one great power after another.

Yet Hebrew writers and historians saw more to it than this. They traced their national history back to slavery in Egypt. It was God's great act of deliverance that had freed them, through the agency of his servant Moses, and had given birth to their nation. It was their God who had helped them to escape from their enemies; and the invasion of Canaan was seen as a crusade.

In Canaan the nomadic wanderings ceased and a monarchy was established. The historians felt that God intended them to have this land. It was therefore a 'Promised Land', and, since God seemed to have some definite purpose to achieve through the Hebrew people, they were in a special sense his 'Chosen People'. This strong sense of vocation dominated all Hebrew history and literature.

Old Testament history had therefore a very obvious religious bias. The divine plan for Israel developed from, and was traced back to, God's promise to Abraham, the father of the nation. Every victory against an enemy was a victory for God over the gods. Every defeat was due, not to God's weakness, but to man's unfaithfulness, and was therefore divine punishment. God allowed them to be defeated.

Hebrew historians sought a divine explanation for everything that happened, good or bad. The true explanation might seem to us to be a very simple one, but not to them. A disaster, natural or military, was a sign of God's anger; a narrow escape meant that he had 'repented' or thought better of inflicting some punishment.

The kings of Israel and of Judah were judged by the historians not according to their political ability as rulers, but according to their promotion or neglect of Yahweh worship. If they let it lapse, they 'did what was evil in the sight of the Lord'. Those who did 'what was right' were those who discouraged Baal worship.

Old Testament history, in its present form, comes to us through editors belonging to the surviving Southern Kingdom of Judah. There is therefore, when recording history, a definite bias against the break-away Northern Kingdom of Israel. The Southern Kingdom of Judah maintained kings of the House of David, the north did not.

From the point of view of the south, especially after the Deuteronomic Reform of 621 B.C. (see p. 7), the religion of the north was not approved; for there, Yahweh was not worshipped in Jerusalem (which belonged to the south) but at the rival shrines of Dan and Bethel. The disapproval, however, is that of historians writing retrospectively after the Deuteronomic Reform a whole century after the Northern Kingdom had fallen to the Assyrians in 721 B.C.

As no king of Israel had attempted to bring the north into line with Judah, the southern editors disapproved of them all for 'doing what was evil'. Even King Jehu, who had tried to promote the worship of Yahweh and to overthrow Baal worship in the north, was still at fault because he did not close down the northern shrines (2 Kings 10^{28-31}). It is with a sense of satisfaction that the historians record their eventual closure by King Josiah as part of his reform (2 Kings 23^{15-20}).

Although so many historians, chroniclers, editors, compilers, and writers were responsible for the library which we know as the Old Testament, the unity of their purpose, and the unity of their writings, is remarkable. For the Old Testament is a collection of books, not specially commissioned for the purpose, with authors separately asked to write on a set theme, but naturally developed as the history and literature of a unique nation.

The Deuteronomic Reform

Of all dates in Hebrew history that of the Deuteronomic Reform in 621 B.C. is vital for the student. Not only was it an important landmark in Hebrew religious history, but its far-reaching effects greatly influenced the way in which future historians presented their work.

In 621 B.C., during some repairs to the Temple, a law book was found and shown to the king. King Josiah realized that conditions in Judah fell very far short of the ideals set forth in the newly discovered book. It inspired him to institute a reform based upon those ideas. After reading the laws at a public gathering, he set about removing from his kingdom all shrines to foreign deities, all 'high places' where Yahweh worship and Baal worship were confused, and all persons responsible for promoting such worship, as well as those who practised magic and necromancy (2 Kings 22^3–23^{24}).

Josiah's reform was evidently not confined to his own kingdom of Judah. The Northern Kingdom of Israel, consisting of breakaway tribes, had fallen to Assyrian attacks in 721 B.C., a century before Josiah's reform began. Subsequently, the Assyrians had recolonized the north with a mixed population. The newcomers had converted the existing shrines into places of worship for their own gods: only that at Bethel had been officially kept as a temple for Yahweh. He was regarded as the God of the land. Now all these northern shrines, including Bethel, were destroyed by King Josiah (2 Kings $17^{24–41}$, $23^{15–20}$).

The closing down of all shrines and high places was part of the most significant change of all, that of centralizing sacrificial worship at the Temple at Jerusalem. Hitherto, people had worshipped Yahweh at local shrines and high places, and all meat eaten had first to be offered in sacrifice. The insistence upon the Temple as the only place for sacrifice to Yahweh did much to counteract the confusion between Yahweh and Baal at the high places.

The majority of scholars believe that there is good reason to suppose that the law book found in the temple was the book of Deuteronomy, for Josiah's reforms reflect its law (cf. Deuteronomy $12^{2–19}$, $16^{1–7}$, 17^3, $18^{10, 11}$). For this reason his reform is alternatively known as the Deuteronomic Reform.

It is not known who wrote the book of Deuteronomy, or for how long it lay hidden before its discovery. One theory is that it was written in the Southern Kingdom, during the reign of the wicked king Manasseh, who encouraged all forms of foreign worship. Another suggestion is that it originated in the north, and, upon the downfall of Israel, was brought to Judah by refugee priests from Yahweh's temples at Dan and Bethel. Either way, the time was not then favourable for its publication.

7

The name of the book means 'second law', and it is a restatement of some earlier laws, together with some newer laws reflecting the growth of a much more humanitarian attitude as the centuries had passed. The laws are all put into the mouth of Moses immediately prior to the entry into Canaan. Some of the laws may in fact date back to Moses.

All Hebrew Law is known as the Law of Moses, although he did not write it all. He was the great lawgiver, and all legislation in the spirit of Moses was regarded as Mosaic. It was therefore the authority of Moses, believed to be behind the book of Deuteronomy, which made King Josiah act upon it. It is this that makes it one of the major components of the Pentateuch (see p. 50).

The Deuteronomic editors

The influence of the book of Deuteronomy was very great, not only upon prophets such as Jeremiah and Ezekiel, but upon the later editors of Hebrew history. During the Exile, editors re-compiled their nation's history in the light of Deuteronomy.

The law of the central sanctuary (Deuteronomy 12$^{5-7}$) was taken to refer to the Temple at Jerusalem, for it was there that the law book was found, though in fact Jerusalem was not specifically named. The Deuteronomic editors particularly show the influence of this law by their attitude towards all Yahweh worship other than in the Temple at Jerusalem, even when they wrote about events which had taken place long before the promulgation of Deuteronomy.

This back-dating by the editors of Deuteronomic ideals shows especially in their mentions of the Yahweh temples in the Northern Kingdom. Very harsh is their judgment upon Jeroboam, the first king of the north and responsible for establishing them.

After the death of Solomon in 930 B.C., and the subsequent division of the kingdom into the Northern Kingdom of Israel, consisting of ten breakaway tribes, and the Southern Kingdom of Judah, King Jeroboam had established two national shrines for Yahweh worship in the north. One of the two northern shrines was at Bethel, an ancient sacred place since the time of Jacob's vision. The other shrine was further north at Dan. In each shrine Jeroboam set a golden calf, representing Yahweh, saying, 'Behold your gods, O Israel, who brought you up out of the land of Egypt' (1 Kings 12^{28}' ^{29}). He established a new priesthood, and festivals were held at different times from those in Judah (1 Kings 12$^{25-33}$). Thus the editors refer to him as 'Jeroboam the son of Nebat, who made Israel to sin' (1 Kings 15^{30}' ^{34}, 16^2; 2 Kings 15^{24}, 17^{21}, 23^{15}).

In addition, therefore, to the natural political feeling of southern historians towards the leader of the rebel tribes of the north, there is the religious condemnation based on Deuteronomy and its law of the central sanctuary. Jeroboam acted 300 years before this law was discovered, but nevertheless by Deuteronomic standards he was guilty. He was judged by a later age, and by a more advanced spiritual outlook.

Politically Jeroboam was very able, and his work for King Solomon had brought him into close contact with the dissatisfied subjects. The prophet Ahijah encouraged him to aim at rival kingship. Solomon was aware of the growing support for Jeroboam, who fled to Egypt for safety. Upon Solomon's death, Jeroboam returned as the obvious leader of the rebel tribes (1 Kings 11[26-40], 12[1-5]).

Jeroboam, however, was not responsible for the fact that they were rebels. The northern tribes had never been close in their ties with the stronger tribe of Judah. To them Judah seemed to be over-favoured, for Jerusalem, the capital, although a captured city, became part of Judah's territory; the Temple was built there; and the monarchy showed signs of being exclusive to the tribe of Judah. Solomon's heavy taxation, with promise of its continuance by his son, was the last straw, and the immediate cause of rebellion.

But it was Jeroboam's religious policy, not his politics, that angered the Deuteronomic editors. Yet how guilty was he by the religious standards of his own day? There was no reason why he should not establish temples for Yahweh worship in his kingdom. Bethel was the place where Yahweh had made covenant with Jacob. It was probably not very wrong in his day to represent Yahweh as a calf, for in an agricultural community a bull calf was a symbol of strength. In the north, moreover, agricultural festivals might well need to differ a little from those in the south, as seasons varied slightly.

There is an interesting connection between the mention of Jeroboam's golden calves, and the mention of that said to have been made by Aaron, Moses' brother, during the wanderings in the wilderness (Cf. 1 Kings 12[28] and Exodus 32[4]). The action is very similar, and the suggestion has been made not only that Aaron's action had to be condemned in order that Jeroboam's action could be, but also that Moses himself might have been responsible for the golden calf in the wilderness, there being then nothing disrespectful to Yahweh in representing him in that way. If Moses had done that, then Jeroboam could not be condemned.

The oldest version of the Ten Commandments merely says, 'You shall make for yourself no molten gods' (Exodus 34[17]), which would not exclude the making of an image of Yahweh. It is the later editions of the Ten Commandments (Exodus 20[4] and Deuteronomy 5[8]) which forbid the making of the likeness of anything in heaven or earth. Even there, the ban applies directly only to the worshipping of such likenesses as though they were gods other than Yahweh.

As a matter of fact the Hebrews were not interested in making visible representations of Yahweh. The Ark of the Covenant was their nearest approach, and that was merely a reminder of God's presence. Other peoples made images of almost anything known, and worshipped them as gods. Thus such a practice was associated with foreign cults, and not encouraged. Moreover, as the awareness deepened of Yahweh as the Creator of the Universe, no image of anything within it was adequate to represent him. Prophets like Jeremiah scorned image worship, but then he too was influenced by Deuteronomy.

Jeroboam's shrines at Dan and Bethel would not have been strong enough in their influence when, fifty years later, Queen Jezebel tried to suppress Yahweh worship in the north, and introduce there the cult of Melkart, the Baal of Phoenicia, her own home land (1 Kings 16[29-33]), had not the prophet Elijah fought against this threat and won (1 Kings 18[4, 18-40]). But for him, Yahweh worship might have become extinct in the north.

Although Jeroboam had intended no act of disloyalty to Yahweh, he had nevertheless helped the growth of corrupt religious practices in the north. His golden calves helped to confuse Yahweh and Baal.

The same confusion was also rife in the south. The Temple at Jerusalem was used for foreign cults, since Solomon himself had made provision for the various religious requirements of his numerous foreign wives. The Deuteronomic Reform sought to put an end to this confusion in the south, before proceeding to purge the north.

The Northern Kingdom had three great prophets, all living before the Deuteronomic Reform, and therefore not influenced by it in their attitude towards northern religion.

The first of these prophets, Elijah, has already been mentioned. He did not condemn the shrines at Dan and Bethel, but then it can be said that he was far too concerned about the whole future of Yahweh worship to issue any judgment upon Jeroboam.

Amos (prophesying 760–746 B.C.) was a man from Judah who came to Bethel on business. He might therefore have been expected to be prejudiced against the north; yet he did not condemn the north for worshipping Yahweh at places other than Jerusalem. It was not the religion of the north as such that he criticized, but the fact that religious practice there was isolated from social righteousness.

Amos' words give a picture of Yahweh worship as being correctly observed and performed, but of God as not accepting it because – without social justice – it was worthless. And so Bethel would be destroyed with all else. In the course of his denunciations the priest of

Bethel told Amos to go back to Judah and prophesy there, but Amos had not excluded Judah from his warnings (Amos 2^{4-16}, $4^{4, 5}$, $5^{4, 5}$, 7^{10-13}).

Hosea, prophesying a little later than Amos (746–734 B.C.), was a native of the north. He was very concerned at the corruption of the north because of the prevalence of Baal worship, and condemned the priests for encouraging this state of affairs. In the name of God, he said, 'I have spurned your calf. . . . A workman made it; it is not God. The calf of Samaria shall be broken to pieces' (Hosea 8^5). It was thus that Hosea condemned the shrine at Bethel: it had become corrupt, and no longer worthy of Yahweh.

The condemnation by the prophets was, however, different from that of the Deuteronomic editors. Both south and north were plagued by Baal worship until the Deuteronomic Reform took drastic steps to curb it. The prophets did not condemn Jeroboam as did the Deuteronomic editors, nor did they object to other places for Yahweh worship, for this was usual. The prophets condemned corrupt religion wherever it was centred, in the north, or at Jerusalem.

Examples of Deuteronomic editorial comment may be seen in Judges 2^{11-19}, $3^{7-10, 12-15}$, 4^{1-3}, 6^{1-10}, 8^{33-35}, 10^{6-16}, 13^1. The story in chapter 18 was probably included in order to show contempt for the shrine at Dan.

In the books of Kings references to all the northern kings as 'doing that which was evil' and following in the ways of Jeroboam, are later editorial comments; and there is strong Deuteronomic influence in the following accounts: 1 Kings 8^{14-61}, 13^{1-10}, $14^{7-11, 13-16}$; 2 Kings 17^{7-end}, 23^{15-20}.

The construction of Hebrew history

Most students at one time or another have been engaged upon a project of some kind. Imagine making a special study of the town in which one lives, and compiling a history of it. Many sources of information would be available.

Existing history books would be a guide for a start. One might wish to include some extracts in the project, and also make some amendments. The town archives, or local branch of the Record Society, would provide original documents, charters, court rolls, manor rolls, etc., which could be copied, or partly copied, and included in the study. Special articles by local people, stories from the past, local traditions, poetry, music, pictures, maps would all help. The local newspaper would also furnish accounts of important events, and of visits by eminent people. One might

11

well find more than one account of some event, and these might not agree in detail. This would present a problem – which account to take. Having gathered all the material together, one would be ready to begin writing. When completed, this local history would be quite a collection of information from a wide variety of sources, some of it written by oneself, some of it copied exactly from original documents, some of it perhaps cut out and mounted. All the sources would be linked together by one's own comments and points of view as historian.

This is but a simple comparison with the processes involved in the compilation of Old Testament history. The processes did not take place once, but over and over again, editing and re-editing occurring for nearly a thousand years. It is the task of the expert to try to recognize the various sources, and the editorial comments (often revealing strong religious points of view), and to unravel the processes of compilation.

At first this might appear to be of small value, but biblical interpretation can be profoundly affected by the results. A single example will make this clear. The Creation parable of Genesis 1, according to most scholars, does not come from an early source, but from a priestly exilic one, around 500 B.C. So, too, does the reference to it in the Decalogue of Exodus 20[11].

Again, an editor using mainly a prose source may have inserted an appropriate verse or two of poetry. It is important to know when this has been done, for, while a prose chronicle may be accepted factually, poetry cannot always be regarded in this way. In the more recent editions of the Bible the poetry is easily recognized by the reader, because it is printed in verse form (e.g. Numbers 21[17, 18, 27-30]; Joshua 10[12, 13]).

In a modern history book the author usually makes it quite clear when he is quoting from a source, by the use of quotation marks, and by giving due acknowledgment. There was no copyright law for the Hebrew historian, no quotation marks. The mention of a source was quite optional. Sometimes, however, sources were mentioned. For example, the Chronicles of the Kings of Israel (2 Kings 14[15]); the Chronicles of the Kings of Judah (2 Kings 15[36]); the Book of the Law of God (Joshua 24[26]); the Book of the Wars of the Lord (Numbers 21[14]); the Book of Jashar – a collection of poems and songs (Joshua 10[13]; 2 Samuel 1[18]).

In addition to these official court records, the Hebrew historian or editor had many other written sources available to him, but now lost to us. From the time of Moses there is mention of matters being written down (Exodus 24[4]; Deuteronomy 31[24]). Some very early material has probably thus got caught up into the present Old Testament.

Oral traditions, customs, folklore, popular stories and legends about national heroes, national songs, all have been incorporated into Hebrew history. Together with the history have been preserved the biographies and autobiographies of prophets, and numerous literary works written to convey or commend particular ideas (see p. 61).

The Pentateuch (i.e. the first 'five books' of the Old Testament), for the Jew the most important part of the Jewish Scriptures, has been subjected by scholars to very careful analysis, in order to discern its main sources. These are four, each incorporating even older material.

(1) *The Jehovistic source* (950–800 B.C.)

This source is so called because of the Hebrew name used in it for God, Jehovah or Yahweh (see p. 25). In English Yahweh is translated as 'the Lord'. Because the name used for God is one of this source's main characteristics, it is referred to as source or document J. It originates from the Southern Kingdom of Judah.

Source J preserves for us the account of the Creation beginning at Genesis 2^{4b}, the parable of Adam and Eve (Genesis 3), the call of Abraham and God's promise to him and the finding of a wife for Isaac (Genesis 24), the Burning Bush (Exodus 3^{2-12}), and the Decalogue (Exodus 34).

(2) *The Elohistic source* (800 B.C.)

This source is so called because the Hebrew word used in it for God is *elohim*, the plural of *el*, meaning 'a god'. In English *elohim* is translated as 'God'. Because the word used for God is one of the main characteristics of this source it is referred to as source or document E. It originates from the Northern Kingdom of Israel.

Source E preserves for us the story of Hagar and Ishmael (Genesis 21^{6-34}), the projected sacrifice of Isaac (Genesis 22^{1-14}), Joseph's adventures in Egypt (Genesis 40–42, 45), the birth and preservation of Moses (Exodus 1^{15}–2^{10}), and the Book of the Covenant (Exodus 20^{22}–23).

(3) *The Deuteronomic source* (621 B.C.)

This source is so called because it consists mainly of the book of Deuteronomy. It was discovered during the reign of King Josiah (see p. 50).

(4) *The Priestly sources* (500 B.C.)

This source, referred to as P, was compiled by Jewish priests in Babylon. They looked at history from a priestly point of view, and so were particularly interested in all historical events which had any bearing on the development of the practices of Hebrew religion.

The whole of the book of Leviticus, a manual of laws for priests, and much else in the Pentateuch, comes to us from these priestly writers and historians: for example, the Creation parable (Genesis 1–2^{4a}) giving

13

extra sanctity to the Sabbath, Abraham's circumcision (Genesis 17) and his son's (Genesis 21[4]), Abraham's purchase of a burial place (Genesis 23), the origin of the divine name (Exodus 6[2]–7[13]), the Passover ritual (Exodus 12[1–20, 40–51]), the construction of the Tabernacle, the appointment of priests, and the making of the Ark of the Covenant (Exodus 25–31, 35–40), the numbering of the tribes (Numbers 1–10), and the greater part of the book of Numbers (Numbers 15, 19, 25[6]–31, 33–36).

The very elaborate laws in the Pentateuch concerned with ritual and ceremonial are the work of the priests. Chapters 17–26 of the book of Leviticus are known as the Code of Holiness. The section receives its name because of the stress it lays upon the need for holiness – 'You shall be holy; for I the Lord your God am holy' (Leviticus 19[2]). The chapters may well have once formed a separate document. The section is sometimes referred to as H, although now it is part of P.

By a complicated process of editing and re-editing, especially during the Exile and after, these separate sources became combined. Often two versions of an incident would be woven together. The story of Noah is a mixture of sources J and P (Genesis 6[9]–9[29]). Source P says that two of each living creature should go into the ark (Genesis 6[19]), but source J says seven of some (Genesis 7[2–3]). According to the J account, Joseph was sold by his brothers to Ishmaelites, while an insertion from E says that they were Midianites (Genesis 37[25, 28]).

The Ten Commandments appear in the Pentateuch three times over. Source J provides the Decalogue in Exodus 34[14–26]. Many scholars believe this to be the oldest version. The Deuteronomic Decalogue is to be found in Deuteronomy 5, and is of much later date. It bears a strong resemblance to the traditional, and generally better known, Decalogue of Exodus 20, which is basically from document E but with additional material from J and P.

Eventually the material compiled from these various sources was divided into the five 'books of Moses' and given their present names:

Genesis – meaning origin, material giving the origins of the human race in general, and the Hebrew nation in particular.
Exodus – meaning departure, material giving the account of the exodus from Egypt, and the making of the Covenant.
Leviticus – a name derived from the priestly tribe of Levi (Source P).
Numbers – so named because of the census of Hebrew tribes reported in chapters 1–10.
Deuteronomy – meaning second law, being a restatement of many earlier laws (Source D).

3. Hebrew Belief in God

The way in which he is written about

The two-way process of man's search for God, and God's revelation of himself to man, is the most important of all the themes to be found in that library of books which we call the Old Testament. It is the theme that links together a wide variety of books and types of writing.

It was the firm conviction of the Hebrew historians that God, instead of making himself known to the whole world, decided to reveal himself first to a select few, chosen for that purpose and thus in a very special sense *his* people When he was known to them, they could in turn bring others to know him. This process of 'religious education' by God covers well over a thousand years.

In early days the Hebrew understanding of God was very primitive indeed, for they believed that he must have the same characteristics as other gods, be pleased with the same sort of barbaric reverence, be superstitiously offended by the same omissions, and react with the same sort of spiteful anger. Thus a near miss from a threatened disaster could be regarded as God's repenting of an evil which he was proposing to do; and God was written about in a primitive way by people who had as yet a very limited knowledge of him.

This may seem quite obvious to some, but it is surprising how many normally intelligent people, inheritors of 2000 years of the Christian revelation of God, expect to find the same advanced knowledge possessed by the people of the Old Testament. It is most important to realize that people wrote about God as they understood him in their own day. This is precisely what twentieth-century theologians are doing now. God himself does not change, but man's understanding grows and deepens.

One would expect St. John and St. Paul, for example, to have a rather fuller understanding of God than had Abraham, who thought that he would be pleased by human sacrifice; or Joshua, who was quite sure that the destruction of a whole city, men, women, and children included, was a divine command (Joshua 8[1, 2], 10[40]). Human sacrifice and wholesale slaughter by this pretext were common in their day, and they had yet to learn otherwise.

Therefore to expect every Old Testament reference to God to be as profound as those of a New Testament author is even more foolish than to expect to find a sixth-form essay or university thesis in an infant school.

A major misunderstanding of the Old Testament idea of God is caused by a failure to appreciate the varied types of writing used by those who are describing him. Yet, as in other literature due allowance is made for the particular method of expression, so it should be here. For example, whereas in modern literature Robinson Crusoe reads like autobiography but is regarded as fiction, so in the Bible the book of Jonah reads like biography but is best regarded as allegory (see p. 69).

The Old Testament is the drama of a nation. The events are told with dramatic force in simple bold style. The words are put into the mouths of the characters, and need hardly any rewriting to present them in the form of a play (e.g. Exodus 5–14: the drama of the Exodus). In this dramatic style of writing God also is given his script (cf. Medieval Mystery Plays). His lines were often not worthy of him, but they were the best that the authors could do with their limited knowledge (e.g. Exodus 8¹: 'Let my people go, that they may serve me. But if you refuse to let them go, behold, I will plague all your country with frogs'; see also Exodus 14²¹⁻²³, 9¹³⁻¹⁹, 11¹, ², 12¹², ¹³, 14¹⁵⁻¹⁸).

This device by Hebrew writers of expressing religious ideas in the first person singular, and putting them into the mouth of God, appears widely in the drama of the Old Testament as a whole. A person with a strong conviction would thus not write or say 'I think' or 'in my opinion' but 'The Lord says, go and do. . . .' (e.g. Numbers 33⁵⁰⁻⁵⁶; Joshua 7¹³; 1 Samuel 15², ³). It is a style that one would hesitate to use today, though a forceful preacher might put over his message in this way: 'God is saying to us, "Why are you spending so much money on war when half my people are starving?" '

The prophets, particularly, regarded themselves as the mouthpiece of God. God's word came to them, and was expressed through them, and with such conviction that they could proclaim, 'Thus saith the Lord', and then, in the first person singular, write their message as spoken directly by God. The inspiration was undoubtedly God-given, but their words are human words reflecting their human beliefs. The stern Amos writes of a stern God, and the forgiving Hosea speaks of a merciful God.

Unless one stops to think about this style of writing, one may develop a vague idea that God was in some way broadcasting to the Hebrews, that they actually heard his voice, and wrote down his words with the accuracy of a tape-recorder.

The Bible has rightly been called the Word of God, but it is the 'word' of his inspiration, as he reveals himself more and more to his people. They ascribe words to him, according to the measure of their understanding of his 'words' to them. At the same time some of the words given to God are so profound that divine inspiration is hard to doubt.

A notable example of such inspiration is to be found in the writings of the unknown prophet of the Exile, usually referred to as Deutero (or Second) Isaiah, contained in chapters 40–55 of Isaiah. This prophet was convinced that God was the Universal Creator, and that no other gods existed. These are some of the words that he gives God to say:

Thus says the Lord, the King of Israel
and his Redeemer, the Lord of hosts:
'I am the first and I am the last;
besides me there is no god. . . .' (Isaiah 44[6])

It had taken the Hebrews about a thousand years from the time of Moses to be able to give God such lines in their drama.

How often, even after 2000 years of Christianity, do we still tend to imagine God as having our outlook upon things. We assume him to have our nationality, to belong to our political party and to our particular Christian denomination; to approve of the things of which we approve; to disapprove of the things that we do not like; and, of course, to be a firm ally if we engage in a military campaign. The early Hebrews can be forgiven if they thought of God in similar ways.

An illustration is afforded by Samuel. He disapproved of the Hebrews request for a king. He took it personally. He was therefore quite sure that God disapproved also. A rather hurt Samuel prayed to God, and felt that he, Samuel, was not alone in his rejection by the people. Rejecting him was the same as rejecting his God (1 Samuel 8[1–10]).

Also it was felt that God was primarily a Hebrew, and that other peoples were not much his concern. Some prophets began to think that God had power over other nations; but even in the time of Jesus such anger was caused by his suggestion that God was also concerned with people other than Jews, that Jesus was nearly killed (Luke 4[25–30]).

The words sometimes given to God by Hebrew writers reflect their own fierce nationalism, which increased markedly after the Exile, keeping Jews apart from Gentiles. Thus the death of some Egyptians in the course of the Exodus, the slaughter of some Amalekites (1 Samuel 15[3]), the massacre of the prophets of Baal by Elijah (1 Kings 18[40]) were all believed to be approved by God, for the slaughtered belonged to enemy nations and a disapproved religion.

This Old Testament cruelty ascribed to God, and put into his script, should not be judged from a Christian standpoint; and it should perhaps be remembered that Christians also have made the same mistakes. It is one of the sad features of Christian history that cruelty and intolerance have figured so prominently in the relationships between varying groups of Christians, and still linger on. The Hebrews had far less to guide them.

17

Finally, how is the value of the utterances ascribed to God in the Old Testament to be assessed? What utterances can be regarded as worthy script, and what utterances disclose an outgrown concept of God? The key lies in the New Testament.

Christians believe that Christ's revelation of the character of God superseded all that went before. He was God's final act of revelation of himself. All therefore in the Old Testament which is completely out of line with Christ's revelation shows not God as he is, but the imperfect seeking after God. Much in the Old Testament comes very close to the New Testament picture of God; but some is so different that at least one of the early heresies that threatened the Christian Church, the Marcionite, proclaimed an Old Testament God as distinct from a New Testament God.

Some people still find it hard to grasp that God does not change, but that human understanding of him increases. Furthermore, whatever lines were ascribed to God, worthy or not, they are none the less a forceful reminder of that sense of divine purpose which makes the outlook of Hebrew writers unique. No other inspiration would make it quite so compelling.

The first thousand years of Hebrew history

It is very difficult to trace an actual awareness of the Hebrew's God, Yahweh, before Moses felt called by him to go to help in the Hebrew slaves' escape from Egypt. The slaves, a nation in the making, needed a god to protect their interests. At Sinai Moses introduced them to the god who had helped them to escape. He agreed to be their god if they would be his people. Thus the Exodus and the Covenant are the first formal recognition of Yahweh by the Hebrews.

But was God known before this? It seems more than likely that Moses learned about him from his father-in-law, Jethro, a priest of Midian. This seems to point to the possibility of Yahweh's already being the God of the Midianites. According to Exodus 6[3] before the call of Moses God was not known by the name Yahweh, translated 'the Lord' (see p. 25. Inscriptions found by archaeologists do indicate that various forms of the name were not unknown in ancient times.

The Hebrew historians looked back upon the Exodus as Yahweh's greatest achievement. This was the birth of their nation, the Chosen People. They tried therefore to trace the workings of Yahweh back to before the Exodus. It was not only part of God's plan that these people should be brought from Egypt, but perhaps it was also Yahweh's working that first brought them there.

Hebrew national history begins with the Exodus, but what might be called Hebrew *pre-national* history is to be found in the book of Genesis in the stories of the Patriarchs, and in their tribal movements within that area known as the 'fertile crescent'. Abraham's tribe left Ur, at one end of the fertile crescent, travelled north to Haran, and thence south into Canaan. Thence again Jacob and his sons finally arrived in Egypt.

For those with so strong a conviction of being God's Chosen People, these events were not just chance. The historians felt that God called Abraham and promised great things for his descendants, and that God continued to reassure the Patriarchs to the same effect. A new land would be given to them, and a great people would result from them. Moreover, the divine purpose for them was that they should be a blessing to all the world.

Thus the book of Genesis forms a prologue or overture to Hebrew national history, setting out in miniature God's plan for the future nation and for the world.

(a) *The Patriarchs*   In the time of the Patriarchs God was at first merely one *el* (god) among many, but gradually he began to emerge distinct from others. People believed in the existence of many *els* or *elohim* (plural). Sometimes an *el* would make his presence known at a particular spot – a tree, or a spring, or a stone. He would then be referred to as the *el* of that particular spot. Having acquired a name, he then ranked as a more important *el*.

In the patriarchal stories God is first an *el* among many who made himself known at certain sacred places. Jacob's vision of him caused Jacob to name the place of the vision Beth-el, that is, house of God, and God was then El-Beth-el, that is, the God of Beth-el. He was an *el* who had acquired a name (Genesis 28^{19}, 35^{7}).

Whether God was ever a tribal god in the time of the Patriarchs is uncertain. Abraham and his people came from Babylon, where the moon god was worshipped, to Haran, where there was a temple for moon worship. Abraham's main religion was probably that of moon worship. This influence has always been strong in Judaism, even down to the present Jewish calendar. However, God, or El, or Elohim, or el-Shaddai (i.e. God Almighty) seemed to be shaping the destiny of the Patriarchs, whether or not his work was acknowledged by them.

When God called Moses to go to help his people, it was as the God of Abraham, Isaac and Jacob that he presented himself. Either Moses, or the historians, or both, were convinced that the Exodus was not God's first interest in Hebrew affairs.

For centuries an anthropomorphic idea of God was to prevail. This means that he was thought of as a sort of super-human being, with eyes, ears, arms, hands etc. and emotions just like a human being. The person

19

who wrote that God made 'man in his own image' was thinking like this (Genesis 1^{26}).

(*b*) *The wanderings in the wilderness* From the solemn Covenant at Mount Sinai to the invasion of Canaan, Yahweh was the tribal God of all the tribes involved in the Exodus. He had shown himself to be a 'man of war' (Exodus 15^3) by his conquest of the pursuing Egyptians at the Red Sea. He was a God of the desert which they now inhabited, a God of storm and fire.

From its description in Exodus 19, Mount Sinai (the real one, not the traditional one) was possibly a volcano, situated somewhere in the land of Midian, where Moses had lived in exile, and where he had received his call. Mount Horeb, the scene of the burning bush story as recorded in document J, is the same mountain (see p. 85).

Many prophets regarded the wilderness period as the time when Yahweh worship was at its best. Contamination with other religions had not yet begun, and loyalty to Yahweh had not yet been put to the test. Jeremiah pictured Yahweh as a husband courting Israel during these early years (Jeremiah 31^{32}).

Whenever danger threatened, the Hebrews understood it to mean that Yahweh might be angry. Moses is shown reminding God that his divine reputation is at stake. What would people say if God failed his own people now, after all that he had done for them? He will seem diminished if the Hebrews are defeated (Exodus 32$^{11-14}$; Numbers 14$^{15,\ 16}$; Joshua 7^9). He is, above all else, the God who brought them out of Egypt and slavery. That act of deliverance was his claim to their loyalty (Exodus 20^2).

(*c*) *The conquest and the settlement of Canaan* The story is told more as a crusade than as an invasion. The Hebrew historians wrote about the conquest with rather more religious zeal than was probably felt at the time by the ordinary people involved, and were ready with reasons to explain the setbacks and delays that plainly occurred.

According to Joshua the conquest was short and sharp; according to Judges it took a long time. History would seem to indicate a period of 200 years from the entry into the Promised Land to the establishment of the monarchy. Yet the historians would never attribute the slowness of progress to any failure of God's power to help. Always it was because the Hebrews themselves had in some way disobeyed God or been unfaithful to him.

Thus, why were the Hebrews so long upon the road? It was not that they were in no hurry. It must be that God was displeased, and was punishing them for cowardice (Numbers 14$^{22,\ 23}$). Why did not the great Moses lead his people to victory? It could not be that he was too old, and his work done, and that a younger man was needed for military conquest. It must be that he too had displeased God in some way – hit a rock, perhaps, instead of speaking to it (Numbers 20⁸⁻¹²). This explanation, from a late priestly source, does not occur in the earlier account from J and E in Exodus 17²⁻⁷. (The explanation is another example of a very primitive conception of God: a god who was thought to be petulant or vindictive presented no moral problems then (see p. 19).)

After the successful capture of Jericho, following a war of nerves, the Hebrews met their first failure at Ai. Here they could not imagine that they were not strong enough, or that God was not strong enough, to capture it (Joshua 7⁴, 8³). Someone had disobeyed what was then thought to be God's command to destroy the city, sparing nothing save the cattle (Joshua 8²). Inquiries soon revealed the offender, Achan, who had taken some plunder for himself. Yahweh had thus been disobeyed.

The subsequent death of Achan was the punishment for his disobedience. The severity of the punishment, involving his family and possessions, is explained by the ancient fear of contact with anything holy, dedicated or taboo (see p. 90).

The cruel notion of carrying out God's supposed wishes by completely destroying an enemy lasted for several centuries. Saul was reprimanded by Samuel for sparing the king of the Amalekites (1 Samuel 15). Later the law was revised a little, but even then only in the case of distant enemies, when the males only were to be killed. The fear that Yahweh worship might become contaminated by heathen practices provided religious justification for slaughter (Deuteronomy 20¹³⁻¹⁸).

The book of Judges shows how often the Hebrews fell into the hands of the enemy tribes already in possession of the land, sometimes for forty years or so (Judges 13¹), until such time as a chieftain or deliverer rose to sufficient power to throw off the oppression. The religious reason given for this misfortune was unfaithfulness to Yahweh: he allowed them to be overcome because they worshipped other gods. When they were penitent he sent them a Judge to set them free (Judges 2¹¹⁻²³).

The conquest of Canaan took place at a time when people believed that the gods belonged to particular territories. Going from one land to another, one went from the jurisdiction of one god to that of another. Yahweh was a God of the desert, and so a problem arose. For Canaan already had gods to look after it. They were agricultural gods, or gods of fertility, whose special concern was with plentiful crops and herds. Every hill top or 'high place' had its shrine, consisting of an altar to the male deity or Baal; and a tree, or wooden pole, or Asherah to the female deity. Some of these Baals had proper names, like Melkart, Milcom, Molech and Chemosh (see p. 23).

The Hebrews entering the land of Canaan would not want to run the risk of offending these gods by ignoring them; and was Yahweh any use when it came to agricultural matters? Better worship both Yahweh and the Baals! Thus Yahweh was worshipped at the same high places as Baal, and for ordinary people the distinction between Yahweh and Baal was very slight.

It was the great task of the prophets to try to keep the distinction, and recall people to the worship of Yahweh only.

The monarchy – from Saul to the Exile

The uniting of the tribes into a nation with its own king did much to keep Yahweh distinct from the Baals. Yahweh was the God of the nation. David brought his Ark of the Covenant to Jerusalem, his newly captured capital. He did much to promote a national shrine for Yahweh, and made plans for a temple, the building of which was carried out by his son Solomon.

This did not stop people from worshipping the Baals, but it was a reminder that Yahweh was their only official God.

Unfortunately, even the Temple was at times not exclusive to Yahweh. It was the chapel royal; and kings, such as Solomon, who made many marriage alliances with other kingdoms, had to make provision for the religious needs of their wives. Shrines to foreign deities thus often marred the Temple.

With the division of the kingdom after the death of Solomon, two more temples were built at sanctuaries already ancient, to provide centres of worship in the Northern Kingdom – one at Dan, and another at Bethel. It was the cry of the prophets that people seemed to think that, provided they gave their formal worship to their official God in his temple, they could then do as they pleased, and worship whatever else they chose to. Yahweh would still be satisfied and stand by them, as they felt he was obliged to do in time of trouble.

When King Ahab of the Northern Kingdom married Jezebel, a princess of Tyre, she sought to promote the worship of Melkart, the Phoenician Baal, in Israelite territory. A temple to Melkart was built in Samaria, the capital. It became fashionable to worship there. Priests of Melkart were brought into Israel by Jezebel to effect a 'take over' from Yahweh. It was Elijah who challenged the right of Melkart to enter Yahweh's land. Elijah did not doubt the existence of Melkart, or any other gods; but he did believe that only Yahweh should be worshipped by his own people.

The later prophets, from Amos onwards, were quickly moving towards a monotheistic idea of God, although until the Exile it was not expressed in so many words. These prophets began to see Yahweh as controlling the destinies and activities of other nations, using them also to fulfil his purpose towards Israel. Thus Isaiah could see God using Assyria as a 'rod' with which to bring Israel to her senses. Amos saw something of God the Creator of the Universe, who made the Pleiades and Orion (Amos 5⁸).

All the major pre-Exile prophets stressed the importance of the covenant relationship between Yahweh and Israel. Hosea and Jeremiah saw it as more than a mere legal contract to be broken without hurt. It was rather like a marriage agreement. Israel was being unfaithful to God, like a bride who despised her husband's gifts and went after other lovers.

The prophets tried to get the people to realize that other gods were no use to them; but the religious beliefs of the prophets were far in advance of those of ordinary people, whose actions were dominated by superstition much more than by theology.

King Josiah's reforms in 621 B.C. helped to preserve the distinction between Yahweh and the Baals. The finding of a law book in the Temple caused the king to close down all high places, and forbid them to be used for sacrifice to Yahweh (2 Kings 23⁸). The Temple in Jerusalem became the only place where such sacrifice could be offered.

The prophets did much to increase man's awareness of the character of God. He was shown to be a God of justice and righteousness, who wanted fair dealing among his people. He was merciful and longing to forgive, if his people would but give him the opportunity. He was a holy God of moral perfection, who wanted his people to be thus holy also.

Together with this growth in knowledge of God, came a growing gulf between man and God. Moses could talk with God, 'man to man' as it were (Exodus 33¹¹); but Isaiah of Jerusalem, a thousand years later, saw the Lord 'high and lifted up', before whom the seraphim covered their faces (Isaiah 6²). Yahweh was now 'the holy One of Israel' – not holy in the old superstitious sense, but holy in his perfection of character, which set him so far apart from man. Such was Isaiah's reaction to his vision of God (Isaiah 6⁵). (The other 'Isaiahs' are distinguished on page 51.)

The Exile

It was the Exile that made the Hebrews realize that God alone was the Creator of the World (Isaiah 44⁶). Their first reaction to exile was that they were separated from God, because they were in a foreign land, and he was left behind. 'How shall we sing the Lord's song in a foreign land?' (Psalm 137⁴.) Then they began to feel that this was not so. Wherever they were, God was supreme.

Consequently, after the first shock, their spirits began to revive; and, helped by the prophets, the faithful among them began to look forward to a return. Plans were made for a new Temple and its services. Hebrew history and law were re-edited. Non-sacrificial worship (later synagogue worship) consisting of readings from the Law and the Prophets was devised; and a new emphasis was put upon the rite of circumcision.

It was during the Exile that an unknown writer produced the 'Songs of the Suffering Servant', four remarkable poems preserved in the book of Isaiah (42^{1-4}, 49^{1-6}, 50^{4-9}, 52^{13}–53^{12}) which form possibly the closest of all links between Old Testament and New Testament theology, for they were greatly to influence Jesus in his role as Messiah. The poems imagine God achieving his purpose through his specially chosen Servant. The writer was not sure whether this Servant was faithful Israel, or a particular individual; but he felt that, in some way, suffering – of the innocent on behalf of the guilty – was to be God's way of redemption. This was an unusual idea, because it was generally assumed that God could prove his greatness only by displays of physical power.

After the Exile

Now that the Hebrews believed in one God the peak of their spiritual development had been reached, although they still had to put this belief into practice. The belief that they were God's Chosen People was stronger than ever, but with the unfortunate result that many of the returned Jews adopted an exclusive, rather than a missionary, policy towards the Gentiles. They wanted to keep themselves to themselves, and God also to themselves. Thus they were missing their vocation to make him known to the rest of the world. The book of Ruth and the book of Jonah were written at this time as a protest against this exclusive attitude (see pp. 68 and 69).

The temptation of Baal worship grew less after the Exile. The fear of displeasing these gods was no longer real, since Yahweh was the only God. Nor were there now many prophets, for the curse of Baal worship was a thing of the past. Jews now had the Law, made specially applicable to them by Scribes, as a guide to behaviour. Judaism steadily acquired a very legal aspect in that it became a religion dominated by laws.

This was both a good thing and a bad thing. It was good because it produced many devout Jews who suffered martyrdom during the latter part of the Seleucid rule of Palestine (198–64 B.C.) rather than break the Law. Unfortunately it also produced the Pharisees of the New Testament who saw the keeping of a law as an end in itself – the way to sanctity.

Belief in life after death, although never the official belief of Judaism

24

(not even for the New Testament Sadducees), increased greatly during this period. Since Yahweh was the Creator of the Universe, nowhere was outside his care. Therefore even the place of the departed was his. Hitherto death had meant separation from God; his rewards to men had to be given in this life. Now there was nowhere one could escape from God. 'If I take the wings of the morning . . .' (Psalm 139⁹).

Those who gave their lives for their faith caused people to think that somewhere God would make it up to them (see p. 102).

Now, too, since God seemed to be rather more remote, there was much more mention of angels, as a means of bridging the gulf between God and men. No longer did he speak quite so directly to men. In this connection the idea of God's Wisdom and God's Word, as his means of communication with his creation, became prominent (see p. 64).

The name of God

The need for a proper name for God no longer exists, for most western people are either monotheist or atheist, or somewhere between the two. The monotheist believes in one God, the atheist does not, but it is the same God who features in their belief or unbelief. Indeed the noun 'god' when spelt with a capital G has become almost a proper noun, and certainly a title for the Supreme Being and Universal Creator.

Philosophers use other terms for God, such as the First Cause, the Ultimate Reality, the Absolute, the Ground of Being; but these are not so much proper names as alternatives for the word 'God', and an attempt to define what that word means. These alternative terms are used because the word 'God' may seem somewhat too restrictive, and its frequent Christian use has in some way limited it, in the western world, to the Christian concept. Other terms therefore are less specifically religious.

The Hebrews needed a name for their God because they lived in polytheistic times. Even when they came to believe in one God, other people did not; and therefore a proper name was needed to distinguish him from the other deities of surrounding peoples, such as Melkart, Milcom, Chemosh, Molech. The Greeks, Romans, and Norsemen also had distinguishing names for their gods.

The Hebrew Old Testament uses various terms for God, and these are represented in English translations in varying ways. Thus *El-Shaddai* is translated as 'God Almighty', *el* being the ordinary noun god, and *shaddai* possibly meaning mountain. *Elohim*, the plural of *el*, is translated as 'God'. This word *el* is one of the major characteristics of the Old Testament source E, giving it the initial letter.

The slightly older source J uses the word Jehovah or Yahweh, which in most English versions of the Bible is translated as 'the Lord'. The

R–C

25

American Revised Standard Version, to which references are made in this book, uses that form. So does the English Revised Version, and so also, almost uniformly, does the Authorized Version. The New English Bible follows the same practice; but the Jerusalem Bible employs the word Yahweh.

Of all the Hebrew words for God, Jehovah 'or Yahweh' is the only one which is a proper name. It is something of a mystery, for it is a name which seems to have evolved from some earlier form at which one can only guess.

The Hebrews had long regarded the name of their God as too sacred for regular use, either spoken or written, for it was not to be taken in vain. When it did come to be written down it appeared as the Hebrew letters for YHWH or JHVH. Written Hebrew had no vowels until the sixth century A.D. By this time it was difficult to know how the name of God had to be pronounced. Such was the reverence shown to the divine name that, although it appeared in writing, it was not actually spoken. Instead the title Adonai, the Hebrew word for Lord, was uttered. When vowels came to be inserted into Hebrew words they were put underneath the existing consonants. In the case of the name YHWH the vowels for Adonai were added, as a reminder to substitute the title for the name.

In English translations this adding of the vowels of one word to the consonants of another gives us the name Yahweh or Jehovah, as the nearest equivalent to the ancient name for God. The technical name for the symbol YHWH is *tetragrammeton* (Greek: 'four letters'). In most English Bibles the word Lord is usually printed in capitals, thus maintaining the Jewish substitute title.

Scholars hold various theories as to how, why, and when YHWH, in some early form, came to be the Hebrew symbol for God. Source J which uses the name YHWH is the oldest major historical source. It dates from the reign of Solomon and therefore indicates that the name was in use then. The question arises, how long had it been in use?

The first mention of it in source J appears in Genesis 4, and seems to indicate that YHWH was a name used before the time of Abraham, and therefore by the Patriarchs. It is impossible to know whether this is due to older source material having been incorporated into source J, or to the back-dating of the use of the divine name by later historians.

The later source E is responsible for giving us the story of Moses' request to God, at the time of his call, for a name (Exodus 3[13-15]). The name given was 'I am who I am' (see R.S.V. margin). This historian was thus trying to explain the origin and meaning of the name YHWH as derived from the Hebrew verb 'to be'. Source E therefore indicates that this name was first used by Moses.

The much later exilic source P insists that God was not known by the name YHWH before the time of Moses (Exodus 6²⁻⁴), but as El-Shaddai – God Almighty. If this is correct, it is possible that Moses learned the name from his father-in-law who was a Midianite priest. There is good reason to suppose that God was already the deity of the Midianite tribe amongst whom Moses had spent his exile from Egypt.

Thus there is a conflict of evidence. It is possible that the E and P historians felt that the call of Moses, and the imminent birth of their nation, was the appropriate place for introducing for the first time the name of the nation's God.

It is also possible that the J historian merely used the name YHWH consistently without regard to the antiquity of his stories. He assumed that, because the name was known to him, it was known also to his ancestors. He was writing stories from the past about the God whom he knew as YHWH, even if they did not.

Hebrew names frequently include the name of God in the form Jah, Iah, or Yah. The prophet Elijah's name contains both the name of God, and the noun *el*, and means 'my God is YHWH', or 'YHWH is God'. This was a name most appropriate in view of Elijah's challenge to Israel resulting in the cry, 'The Lord, he is God' (1 Kings 18³⁹).

Adonijah, the elder brother of Solomon, had a name combining Adonai and YHWH, meaning 'YHWH is my God'; while the prophet Isaiah's name means 'YHWH saves', and Jeremiah's means 'YHWH has appointed'.

These are but a few examples, but it is noticeable that such names do occur after the call of Moses, thus lending weight to the sources E and P theory that this YHWH was not known before the time of Moses.

On the other hand, archaeologists have discovered various forms of the name YHWH (Yahu, Tah, Yave, Ya, Yau, Jah) among peoples other than the Hebrews. The name Jah, as a compound of other names, appears in the Ras Shamra tablets, which originate from a community in Asia Minor of the fifteenth and fourteenth centuries B.C. The Minaean Inscriptions of South Arabia, also probably dating from the fifteenth century B.C., contain the name Jah.

This lends strength to the theory that YHWH was God of the Midianites, and that Moses learned of him through Jethro his father-in-law.

Earlier still are the forms Ya and Yau on Babylonian tablets of 2000 B.C., and the name-compounds of Yave and Yahu found on a tablet at Taanach dated from 2000–1500 B.C. This makes it possible that YHWH was a name for God known to the Patriarchs, as suggested by source J.

A further theory arising from the evidence is that the name YHWH started as a common name or title for a deity before the Hebrews exalted it to prime importance.

4. The Covenant

Its inauguration

The central belief of Hebrew religion was that of a covenant, or contract, between Yahweh and the Hebrew nation. Hebrew historians and theologians were convinced that a very special relationship existed between their people and God. The shaping of their history seemed to indicate that God had a special purpose for them. Even when they came to realize that he was the God who controlled the destinies of other nations, was indeed the Creator of the Universe, still, in a very special sense, he was their possession, and they were his.

The prophet Amos, speaking on behalf of God, expressed the covenant idea thus: 'You only have I known of all the families of the earth' (Amos 3²).

A great event in Hebrew national history marked the inauguration of this contract between Yahweh and Israel. It took place not long after the escape, or exodus, from Egypt, when the Hebrews reached the sacred mountain Horeb, or Sinai. This was the mountain where Moses had felt himself to be in the presence of God, and called by God to rescue his fellow Hebrews from their Egyptian slavery (see p. 85).

Exodus 19 describes the solemn preparations made for a confrontation with God upon the sacred mountain. Moses, in the name of God, said to the people, 'You have seen what I did to the Egyptians, and how I bore you on eagles' wings and brought you to myself. Now therefore, if you will obey my voice and keep my covenant, you shall be my own possession among all peoples; for all the earth is mine, and you shall be to me a kingdom of priests and a holy nation' (Exodus 19³⁻⁶). To this the assembled people made reply, 'All that the Lord has spoken we will do' (Exodus 19⁸).

Thus the promises were made between the two contracting parties. The contract was then 'signed' by the offering of a sacrifice. Moses built an altar at the foot of Mount Sinai and set up twelve pillars representing the twelve tribes. The blood of the sacrifice was sprinkled upon the altar, which represented God. The terms of the contract, the Decalogue and the laws in the Book of the Covenant, were read to the people. Finally the remainder of the blood was scattered over the people. The sacrificial blood sprinkled upon altar and people symbolized the bond that now existed between Yahweh and Israel (Exodus 24³⁻⁸).

This gathering together at Mount Sinai formed the very centre of the Hebrew idea of a covenant relationship between the people and Yahweh. The whole first section of the Bible (the Old Testament) deals with the making of this Old Covenant, and with the working out of the covenant relationship in Hebrew history – God keeping his part of the Covenant, but his people so often not keeping theirs.

Unfortunately the long and established use of the term 'Testament' has tended to obscure this covenant idea, because, whereas the word 'covenant' suggests a joint undertaking, the word 'testament' commonly suggests some person's intention made known before death. The Greek word so translated can carry both meanings: a covenant or a testament is, each in its way, a solemn declaration of intent.

The Covenant People

At Mount Sinai Moses introduced a string of escaped slaves, Hebrew refugees from Egypt, to the God who had made their escape possible. They needed now a God to look after their interests in the future. Yahweh was prepared to adopt them as his people if they would accept him. Their recent escape from Egypt was already enough to assure them that he was capable of being their God.

Unlike the gods of other tribes, Yahweh was not a mere deified ancestor from the past: he was not related to the Hebrews at all. They were convinced that he chose them, although he was quite independent of them. This Covenant was the birth of the future nation. It was a source of unity between a number of tribes, long before any political unity was achieved.

Who were these Hebrews and who were the Covenant People? Hebrew historians probed deeply into the nation's past. Stories and traditions handed down over the centuries pointed to the possibility that, prior to slavery in Egypt, they were a number of related tribes, some of the countless nomadic tribes constantly moving to and fro in the fertile crescent between Egypt, Canaan, and Mesopotamia. Like many others, they had emigrated to Egypt and one of their number, Joseph, had risen to considerable power.

Abraham's father's tribe seems to have been the parent tribe of many later sub-divisions. Even his tribe probably contained Hittite, Amorite, Canaanite and Aramean elements. Yahweh was thought to have played a large part in the tribal movements, especially those of the Abraham, Isaac, and Jacob tribes.

Bible stories always over-simplify the Hebrew origins. Twelve sons of

Jacob move to Egypt, become slaves, and, after what appears to be a short time, twelve tribes march out of Egypt, led by Moses. Twelve tribes assemble at Sinai and enter into covenant with God and become the Covenant People.

But it seems more likely that twelve tribes did not take part in the Exodus. Some members of some tribes did. Many scholars hold that Judah, always the strongest and, ultimately, the surviving tribe, may have left Egypt long before the Exodus; or at least settled in Canaan long before the main Hebrew invasions under Joshua (see p. 20).

As the refugees wandered towards Canaan, they encountered other nomadic tribes. Moses' father-in-law, for instance, was a Midianite priest. From him Moses may have first learned about God. Some of these friendly tribes possibly got caught up with the Hebrews as they journeyed. The Edomites and other Semitic tribes were already in fact distantly related to the Hebrews, being the descendants of Hebrew tribal sub-divisions; but, being of only passing interest to the Old Testament editors, they were given little attention.

After the invasion of Canaan under Joshua, the Covenant was the main thing that the scattered Hebrew tribes had in common for a very long time. When a monarchy was established the king became the guardian of the Covenant. The unique Hebrew conception of monarchy was a result of the Covenant (see p. 44).

All the people over whom the king ruled, whether of the twelve tribes or of other subject states, were Covenant People with a right to its protection and privileges. For example, Ruth the Moabitess married into the tribe of Judah, and thus became a member of the Covenant People. The Gibeonites entered into a special treaty with Joshua, thus acquiring Covenant status – which, when violated centuries later by Saul, required grim retribution (2 Samuel 21[1-14]).

King David's sin of adultery, and of deliberately causing the death in battle of Uriah the Hittite, was aggravated by the fact that the king had violated Uriah's right to Covenant protection. Uriah was married to a Hebrew woman, and the Hebrews were partly of Hittite stock.

Thus many peoples could become Covenant People in much the same way that immigrants to a country often qualify for the benefits of its citizenship.

The Ten Commandments

If asked to think about the origin of the Ten Commandments, most people would recall biblical illustrations of a very aged Moses, staggering down a very steep mountain, and carrying two great paving stones. Biblical films may also come to mind, showing the stones being inscribed in a supernatural manner, and the voice of God dictating through some celestial loudspeaker. Some pictures show Moses, in anger, breaking the stones because he has seen the idolatrous worship of a golden calf started by the Hebrews in his absence.

These mental images are a dramatic over-simplification, and a student must approach the subject of lawgiving on Sinai in a much more mature manner.

The biblical narrative is itself dramatically over-simplified because it marks a highlight in Hebrew history. The consciousness of a special relationship with God, and of a special divine purpose for them, is traced by the Hebrews to this lawgiving. This was where God's Covenant with their nation was made.

Moses had but recently brought a very mixed band of slaves out of Egypt. Already he had to spend much time settling disputes (Exodus 18¹³⁻²⁶). The mixed band had to be shaped into a community, and a community must have some basic rules. Moses realized this, and used religion as his uniting force.

He gathered the people at the foot of Mount Sinai, or Horeb, the mountain where he himself had felt God's call. After making a solemn covenant between Yahweh, the God who had called him, and the people for whom Yahweh seemed to have a special concern, Moses announced the terms of this solemn contract or covenant.

It is interesting to notice how even the most exalted of human beings sometimes feel themselves to be inadequate as an ultimate source of authority. They feel the need to refer to some higher, if not infallible, source of authority, above and beyond themselves or their community. Thus the famous stele of King Hammurabi, the great lawgiver of Babylon, and possibly a contemporary of Abraham, shows him receiving his laws from Shamash, the sun god. Human laws can be questioned, but divine laws not nearly so readily. Some would argue that people have invented their gods, or even God, for this very purpose.

If appeal was not made to a community's god as its source of authority, then the leader or king might be given divine status, which had the same effect of giving to laws a superhuman source. This was so of Roman and Japanese emperors.

And what of Moses? Some might say that he did indeed compile the Ten Commandments by himself. Certainly an audible divine voice and visible divine writing would seem to be a dramatic way of saying that Moses was inspired by God, when compiling a list of basic laws for his rather unruly people. The responsibility of leadership was great for Moses, and the people were often far from being appreciative. He often felt the need to get away from it all, for quiet and opportunity to plan. After one such retreat Moses solemnly announced these divinely inspired laws as the terms of the Covenant.

Were they written on stones? Moses did write things down (Exodus 24[4]). The common form of writing in those days was by making impressions on tablets of wet clay. The Babylonians used a wedge-shaped stick to make their letters upon clay cylinders. It is called cuneiform writing, from the Latin *cuneus*, a wedge. Moses may have recorded his basic rules in this way, or even have engraved them on actual stones from the sacred mountain. It is possible that the stones from the mountain, which were kept in the Ark, were not inscribed at all, but were merely a means of guaranteeing Yahweh's presence with his wandering people. Mount Sinai was Yahweh's home, and stones from the mountain would be part of his home. In that case perhaps clay tablets also were kept in the Ark.

It is not possible now to know exactly what was the form or contents of the Ten Commandments. The lawgiving at Sinai is preserved in the two main Hebrew traditions, source J and source E. Thus there are two accounts of the Covenant and lawgiving recorded in the book of Exodus. The oldest account is to be found in Exodus 34, from source J; the better known account of Exodus 20 is basically the more recent source E.

Much has been added to it by later generations. It is possible that the laws given by Moses were all just very short sentences, as in Exodus 20[13-16]. This is why the Ten Commandments are alternatively referred to as the Decalogue, meaning ten words. In this brief form the Decalogue, at least, may well be the work of Moses.

It is interesting to compare the two Decalogues. The earlier source of Exodus 34 has laws concerning worship only, whereas that of Exodus 20 is remarkable because its laws are both spiritual and social. Although this Decalogue is preserved in a later source, its basic contents could yet be earlier than those of Exodus 34.

An outstanding characteristic of Hebrew Law is the way in which duty to God and duty to man go together. Both formed part of the divine Law, as prophets were quick to remind people if their religion did not express itself in social responsibility. Indeed Jesus' criticisms of the traditions of Scribes and Pharisees was that their rules often obscured the essential spiritual and social basis of the Law.

If the ten short sentences of Exodus 20 do date back to Moses, then the original Ten Commandments set the pattern for future legislation, with their first four commands concerning attitude towards God, and the remainder concerned with one's attitude towards other people. (Sometimes they are divided five and five.) This is perhaps the divine inspiration behind them. Even if it is not the work of Moses, the Decalogue shows that this dual attitude appeared quite early in Hebrew Law.

Some of the commandments in Exodus 20 have been added to as time has passed. Commandment 10 (Exodus 20¹⁷) 'You shall not covet' would not have the words 'neighbour's house' added to it in the nomadic age of Moses. The reason for keeping the Sabbath (Exodus 20¹¹) is a very late addition, being a reference to the Genesis 1 parable of Creation from the exilic priestly source. The Exodus 34 Decalogue contains no such reason (Exodus 34²¹).

The Exodus 20 Decalogue is to be found again in Deuteronomy 5 with two interesting variations: the wife heads the list of the man's possessions, not the house (Deuteronomy 5²¹), and the Sabbath is to be a thankful reminder of the days of slavery in Egypt, when no such rest from work was possible (Deuteronomy 5¹⁵).

A question arises from the two Covenant accounts in the book of Exodus: is the story of Moses breaking the stone tablets merely an editorial device for introducing the second account? It is certainly questionable whether there would be any disapproval of a golden calf representing Yahweh at this early stage in Hebrew history. Later editors disapproved, however, because the rival Northern Kingdom possessed two golden calves in the temples at Dan and Bethel (1 Kings 12²⁸⁻³⁰).

The individual commandments are of interest, even in their shortened form. They are not all original to Moses. He was not the first person to prohibit murder or stealing. Any community would need laws to safeguard its members, their health and their property. This would lead on from murder and stealing to the intent or desire to steal, that is to covet, including a man's wife. Adultery was the stealing of another man's wife.

The Babylonian lawgiver, Hammurabi, who preceded Moses by several centuries, had promulgated a code of laws which could have influenced Hebrew laws (see p. 34).

Of more direct connection with the Decalogue is the influence of the Egyptian Book of the Dead, of about 1500 B.C. Moses may well have been familiar with it. It was a questionnaire placed in a coffin; the soul would be required to give answer to Osiris and the judges of the dead in the Hall of Judgment. The soul had to be prepared to say, 'I have not killed, I have not committed adultery, I have not stolen.'

Although much later than the time of Moses, the seventh-century Babylonian exorcism tablets, known as the *Shurpu*, are of interest. They indicate the way in which a nation's ethical laws develop, probably in tradition and practice long before they actually appear in writing.

The ancient belief that sin caused sickness was still held by the Jews at the time of Jesus, but it was not exclusive to them. The Babylonian Shurpu consisted in part of some questions that a priest would ask the gods in order to find what particular sin was causing an illness. The sins included despising parents, entering a neighbour's house, shedding his blood, stealing his garment, approaching his wife.

The fact that Moses was influenced by existing laws when he compiled his basic commandments does not mean that he merely took other people's ideas. His genius lay in the selection that he made, and the combination of spiritual and social obligations. The Decalogue was meant to be only a foundation for further development.

Textbooks give extracts from these ancient laws, but the complete text of many of them, including the Code of Hammurabi, can be found in *Ancient Near Eastern Texts*, edited by James B. Pritchard.

At the time when Moses and his people entered into solemn covenant relationship with Yahweh, therefore, they were told to put him before all other gods, to worship only him (i.e. monolatry), and to reverence his name and his day. (The Sabbath did not originate with Moses (see p. 114).) Together with this, and of equal importance, were the commands to respect one another's lives and property.

The Book of the Covenant

The basic terms of the Covenant are considered to be contained in the Ten Commandments. In the description of the Covenant ritual (Exodus 24^{3-8}) there is mention of a 'book of the covenant'. The chapters between the account of the Ten Commandments in Exodus 20 and the mention of such a book in Exodus 24 are therefore known as the Book of the Covenant (Exodus $20^{22}-23^{33}$).

The Ten Commandments formed only a nucleus of law, around which considerable expansion would take place. Moses spent much time in lawmaking, and, at the suggestion of his father-in-law, he appointed people to assist him (Exodus 18^{13-26}). This is the way in which law grows as new needs and situations have to be met. The Book of the Covenant, together with the Ten Commandments, is the oldest collection of laws in the Old Testament.

The whole Jewish Law is known as the Law of Moses, though it was certainly not all compiled by him. He started a process which was to grow over the centuries, as do the laws of any country. Moses' Egyptian upbringing, at the heart of the government of a great kingdom, must have helped to prepare him for his future work.

Scholars are unable to date with any certainty the Book of the Covenant. So much of the Old Testament, as we have it now, is a post-exilic re-compilation of previous laws. The Book of the Covenant is preserved, however, in source J, which takes it back to the reign of Solomon. Since source J itself contains older material still, it is possible that the Book of the Covenant forms part of that earlier material. It seems unlikely, though, that it belongs as far back as the time of Moses, for its laws relate mostly to an agricultural way of life, though not as yet a highly organized one. For this reason some scholars ascribe the Book of the Covenant to the period of the Judges.

Hebrew Law did not grow in isolation. It must be remembered that the Hebrew people had for centuries been nomadic tribes, moving to and fro in the fertile crescent of the Near East. This brought them into contact with Babylonian, Canaanite, and Egyptian influences. Nor were the Hebrews the only nomadic tribes. Numerous other peoples were on the move at the same time, and population was hardly ever constant in any one place. When people are moving, so too are ideas and beliefs.

Yet similar ways of life bring similar problems. All communities need laws, however simple. Many laws of such people closely resemble one another. They had dealings with one another for purposes of trade, marriage, or restitution after injury, and this would lead to agreement between tribes on lines of procedure. It is the differences which become significant as the Hebrews advanced spiritually.

The Ark of the Covenant

This was to be a portable shrine, and a visible reminder of Yahweh's presence among his people. Its description is in Exodus 25^{10-22}. It was a chest of acacia wood, overlaid with gold, and surmounted by two gold cherubim facing each other with wing tips touching. The space between the cherubim is called the mercy seat, and it was intended to be a sort of throne for the divine presence.

Two long poles set in rings enabled the chest to be carried. It was said to contain Aaron's rod, a jar of manna, and stones, possibly engraved, from the sacred mountain, Sinai – thus ensuring Yahweh's presence with his people.

The carrying of religious objects and images in procession was no new idea. The Ark of the Covenant, carried by priests, led the Hebrews during their wanderings, and during their invasion of Canaan. It was carried into the river Jordan, and remained there until everyone had crossed safely (Joshua 3); in silent procession it was carried around the walls of Jericho (Joshua 6). When battle against the Philistines was hard going for the Hebrews, Eli's sons brought the Ark from the shrine in Shiloh. A great shout greeted its arrival, and the Philistines were afraid, saying, 'A god has come into the camp' (1 Samuel 4^7).

Unfortunately the Ark was captured by the Philistines, and the shock caused the death of Eli. However, the Ark seemed to bring such misfortune to the Philistines that they were glad to send it back (1 Samuel 6). It was put on to a new cart drawn by two cows, and, divinely guided, it arrived at Beth-shemesh. Sickness broke out among the men of Beth-shemesh, infection no doubt brought from the Philistines by those who had escorted the Ark to the border. The sickness was regarded as a sign of God's displeasure at the undue curiosity that the men of Beth-shemesh had shown.

For a long time the Ark remained at Kiriath-jearim, in the house of Abinadab and his son Eleazar.

When David made Jerusalem his capital he thought that it would be good policy to bring the Ark there. A tragic and rather mysterious story is told (2 Samuel 6^{1-11}) concerning Uzzah, one of the sons of Abinadab, who was accompanying the Ark. When the cart on which the Ark was being carried happened to sway, Uzzah steadied the Ark with his hand, and died suddenly. This was again thought to be a sign of God's anger.

Probably it is an example of the common fear of touching something holy, and thus becoming infected, or maybe the story is only legendary, designed to explain the place name Perezuzzah, which, says R.S.V. margin, means 'the breaking forth upon Uzzah' (see p. 91).

For the time being David abandoned the attempt to bring the Ark to Jerusalem. It remained in the house of Obed-edom the Gittite – another instance of a member of the Covenant People who was not of the twelve tribes.

A later attempt to bring the Ark to Jerusalem was successful (2 Samuel 6^{12-23}), and David himself, as king, led his people in rejoicing and worship, but in a manner that disgusted his wife. He wanted to build a temple to house the Ark, but this task fell to his son Solomon (1 Kings 8^{1-21}).

The prophets and the Covenant

One might have thought that the idea of a covenant relationship with God would be strongest in the Hebrew people during the time of their wanderings, the making of the Covenant being then a recent event. In fact the idea of a covenant grew stronger as time went on. The prophets, who were Israel's theologians, tried to inculcate an awareness of the covenant relationship, and urged Israel to face up to her responsibility as the Covenant People.

Elijah, in the Northern Kingdom, saw the introduction of the Tyrian Baal, Melkart, by Queen Jezebel, as a threat to the Covenant. The people of Israel were being unfaithful to it by following this new and fashionable cult A drought indicated the divine displeasure and Elijah confronted King Ahab, saying, 'You have forsaken the commandments of the Lord and followed the Baals' (1 Kings 18^{18}).

The contest on Mount Carmel proved to the people that their allegiance should be to Yahweh. Elijah and his successor, Elisha, were the instigators of the prophetic revolution in which Ahab and Jezebel were killed, and a massacre of Melkart worshippers purged the kingdom of a foreign threat to the covenant relationship.

With the writing prophets came a new development of thought concerning the covenant relationship. In early religious thought a nation's god was one who looked after its interests, especially in time of war. There were no moral demands made upon the nation. God's relationship with Israel was not like this. There was no obligation on his part to stand by Israel, if Israel disregarded her part of the Covenant agreement. Yahweh could not be 'bought off' by costly worship, and be expected to ignore social injustice and the desire to worship other gods.

Amos tried to make people aware of that. Because they were God's Chosen People he would expect more from them. 'You only have I known of all the families of the earth; therefore I will punish you for all your iniquities' (Amos 3[2]). Judah also is to be punished 'because they have rejected the law of the Lord, and have not kept his statutes' (Amos 2[4]). The Covenant People were not keeping the terms of the Covenant, and yet God was expected to stand by them.

Hosea introduced a more tender note into the idea of the covenant relationship. He saw it, not as a cold legal contract which could be broken without hurt, but more as a marriage contract involving a loving obligation on both partners. Therefore, when Israel was unfaithful to Yahweh, it grieved him as a husband would grieve for an unfaithful wife. Jeremiah developed this still further.

Together with the comparison with the husband and wife relationship, came also the idea of the fatherhood of God, with Israel as his child. Again this is a relationship involving affection on both sides. 'When Israel was a child, I loved him, and out of Egypt I called my son. The more I called them, the more they went from me; they kept sacrificing to the Baals, and burning incense to idols. Yet it was I who taught Ephraim to walk. . . .' (Hosea 11[1-4]).

Isaiah saw God using Assyria as the rod of his anger for chastising Israel (Isaiah 10[5]). After God's judgment a faithful remnant would form the nucleus of a new Covenant People.

Jeremiah believed that, because the Covenant had failed through Israel's unfaithfulness, a new Covenant would be needed. This one God would make in the hearts of men (Jeremiah 31[31-34]).

It is important to realize that the threat of punishment, made by the prophets in the name of God, is not uttered because God is vindictive, but because he loves his people despite their unfaithfulness. The punishment is seen as corrective, God's last resort, as it were, when all other pleading has failed, and the only way to learn becomes the hard way.

Many prophets expressed the hope that Israel would become the spiritual centre of the world, and that other nations would come to know Israel's God. In this way they would become part of the Covenant. This was, as the prophets saw it, the divine plan for the Chosen People. In this way Abraham's family would be a blessing to the world (Genesis 12², 28¹⁴). The Temple would be a 'house of prayer for all peoples' (Isaiah 56⁷).

Nations would say: 'Come, let us go up to the mountain of the Lord, to the house of the God of Jacob; that he may teach us his ways and we may walk in his paths' (Isaiah 2³; Micah 4²); 'Thus says the Lord of hosts. . . . In those days ten men from the nations of every tongue shall take hold of the robe of a Jew, saying, "Let us go with you, for we have heard that God is with you." ' (Zechariah 8²⁰⁻²³.)

It was a tragedy that this universal outlook was not strong enough to prevail. Though the Exile did much to strengthen the Jewish faith, it produced a strong exclusive attitude towards the Gentiles. This was necessary, in a foreign land, if national identity was not to be lost. It was at this time that circumcision became the outward mark of the Covenant and distinguished the Jews from the Babylonians. After the Exile inter-marriage with foreigners was not permitted, and Judaism became insular.

The results of this outlook can well be seen in the New Testament: ceremonial washings by strict Pharisees after touching anything that might have been handled by Gentiles (Mark 7⁴); an attempt made in Nazareth to kill Jesus because he dared to suggest that God was sometimes interested in people who were not Jews (Luke 4²⁵⁻³⁰); St. Stephen stoned to death for saying the same thing (Acts 7).

Thus it was for the Christian Church to form the New Israel, to be the people of the New Covenant. The Old Covenant had failed. Jeremiah's hope was fulfilled by Jesus' death and resurrection. At the Last Supper he said, 'This is my blood of the new covenant which is poured out for many' (Mark 14²⁴). The second part of the Bible is concerned with the making of this new Covenant – hence its name: The New Covenant (see p. 1).

5. The Monarchy

The tribal system

One cannot read the Old Testament without very soon becoming aware of a complicated tribal system underlying Hebrew life. In fact the earlier history of the Hebrews is largely to be seen in terms of tribal migrations, sub-divisions, or amalgamations.

The Scottish clans furnish the comparison nearest or best known to us. The members of a clan would trace their ancestry to some great family of the past. Marriage between members of two clans could cause an amalgamation, or the formation of a new branch of a clan.

Some scholars would see the patriarchal stories of Genesis as nothing more than clan movements, individual personages such as Isaac or Jacob being merely mythical. This is perhaps going too far, but nevertheless the activities of the patriarchs do include their tribes.

The fertile crescent, stretching from the Persian Gulf, up the Tigris–Euphrates valley, down the lowlands of Palestine, and into the narrow cultivated Nile valley, was thickly populated by nomadic tribes. These tribes would stay in one place as long as that place could support them, or until it became too crowded for peaceful existence, and then move on. Sometimes it happened that a tribe became large and powerful enough to rule a wide area, such as Egypt under the Hyksos kings.

The tribe to which Abraham belonged was that of Terah, his father. It stayed for some time in Ur of the Chaldees, near the Persian Gulf. What was the tribal reason for its leaving Ur? The district was very possibly overpopulated, and Terah, a nomadic chief, decided that it was time to move. It is possible also that the move from Ur coincided with the arrival of a new king, Hammurabi, a sun worshipper. Moon worship had been the main religion of Ur, to such an extent as to be almost monotheistic. This could have provided a religious motive for a tribal migration northwards to Haran, where there was a temple to the moon god.

In Haran the first tribal sub-division took place when Abraham, who had for some time been growing rich and powerful, left his father's tribe and journeyed southward into Canaan, taking with him all his relatives, herds and possessions. For a short time famine drove him on

39

into Egypt. Upon his return, his nephew Lot branched off on his own, and another tribal sub-division took place.

When Abraham wanted a bride for his son Isaac, he sent his servant to the parent tribe at Haran to find one of his own people. Rebekah was Abraham's great niece. Abraham's son Ishmael, by his slave wife Hagar, was sent away, and thus was formed the future Ishmaelite tribe.

Rebekah sent her twin son, Jacob, also to Haran to find a bride. He found two, Leah and Rachel, his cousins. After working for a round term of years for his uncle Laban, Jacob wished to break away and form his own tribe, although his uncle was not keen on the idea of supplying him with cattle. Before long Jacob met with his brother Esau, by now the head of the powerful and prosperous Edomite tribe.

Jacob had twelve sons, two by his favourite wife Rachel – Joseph and Benjamin. These twelve became in time the founder tribes of the Jewish nation. Joseph's rise to power in Egypt, and the famine, were the reasons for the migration of Jacob and his sons to Egypt.

The welcome given to them by the Pharaoh supports the view that this migration occurred during the time of the Hyksos dynasty (1800–1600 B.C.). The Hyksos, or Shepherd Kings, were Semitic, that is a tribe thought to be descended from Noah's son, Shem. They were a tribe of the same stock as the Hebrews, and they had risen to power in Egypt. Joseph and his kinsmen were therefore not strangers. Their presence in Egypt helped to strengthen the Hyksos position.

Consequently, when the Hyksos were subsequently expelled from Egypt by the rising to power of the Egyptian Ahmose I, the founder of the XVIII dynasty, the Hebrews in Egypt, rapidly increasing in numbers, were a cause of some concern to this new dynasty. Being related to the previous royal house they were a possible threat to the new regime. Eventually they were reduced to slavery, until Moses and Aaron, of the tribe of Levi, managed to negotiate with the Pharaoh for their release.

The Pharaoh was reluctant to let them go; for, whereas in Egypt they could be kept under subjection, once released to resume their nomadic existence they might become a danger from outside.

After the Exodus the nomadic life of the Hebrews began again. They moved from oasis to oasis, with Moses and Aaron as leaders. Moses did his best to bring some unity to the tribes by getting them all to accept the same deity. During this time, according to the priestly writers, the tribe of Levi became a privileged tribe; for from it alone were drawn the priests and the servants of the sanctuary.

The invasion of Canaan by the tribes took place under the leadership of Joshua, Moses' successor. Two of the tribes, Dan and Issachar, penetrated to the far north. Others were content to settle in the south without going far into Canaan; among these were Simeon and Judah which may perhaps have been there even before the Exodus.

The evidence for this is not easily recognizable, for the history of the conquest and settlement is far more complex than at first appears. Scholars think it quite probable that some Israelite tribes (or perhaps sections of them) were never involved in the Egyptian slavery, and therefore never took part in the Exodus. They may have established themselves in Canaan well before Joshua's invasion.

Judah, for instance, the tribe which survived all others, had already formed alliance with the Canaanites before the period of Egyptian slavery. Some parts of that tribe therefore remained in the Hebron district. Judges 1^{1-19} and Numbers 21^{1-3} show that both the tribes of Simeon and Judah acted independently of Joshua, the latter reference indicating an invasion from the south. Comparatively few representatives of the tribes are said to have migrated to Egypt (Genesis $46^{26, 27}$; Exodus 1^5; Deuteronomy 10^{22}).

The ancient Song of Deborah does not mention all the tribes being called upon to join the alliance, Judah being one of the omissions (Judges 5). The tribe of Asher did not join in (Judges 5^{17}), and archaeological evidence indicates the possibility that it too was established in Canaan prior to the Exodus.

The settlement in Canaan was by no means an easy matter, for the land was already full of other tribes, some Semitic and therefore distantly related, some not; some friendly, and some hostile. For some two hundred years or more there was no political unity among the Hebrews.

Almost contemporary with the Hebrew invasion of Canaan was that of a powerful tribe from across the sea. The Philistines came from Caphtor in Crete, and proved to be a formidable foe to the Hebrews. It was the arrival of the Philistines that made political unity an absolute necessity for the Hebrews, if an effective stand was to be made against these rivals.

The first king of the united tribes was Saul, of the tribe of Benjamin. He was followed by David and Solomon, of the tribe of Judah. David, very wisely, made a newly captured city, Jerusalem, the capital, thus avoiding tribal favouritism.

At the death of Solomon ten tribes broke away and formed the Northern Kingdom of Israel. This powerful kingdom lasted for nearly two hundred years, and was ruled by kings of numerous royal houses. In the Southern Kingdom of Judah there remained only the tribes of Judah and Benjamin, Judah being the dominant tribe.

The south retained the royal line of David, Rehoboam, the son of Solomon, being its first king. As the hope of a Messiah, a second David, grew in people's minds, so too did the importance of preserving the House of David upon the throne.

When the Assyrians conquered the Northern Kingdom in 721 B.C., the majority of the members of the ten tribes were deported. They are sometimes called the ten lost tribes. The remaining kingdom of Judah survived Israel by over a hundred years, and also survived fifty years of exile in Babylon.

It is through Judah that most of Old Testament history continues. Restored after exile, Judah became a nation again, though dominated in turn by Persians, Greeks, Syrians, Egyptians, and Romans. The tribal area was known as Judaea, and its people were known as Jews, whether actually of the tribe of Judah or descendants of the survivors in the north.

The establishment of the monarchy

The establishment of a monarchy was a political necessity for the Hebrews. Widely scattered as they were throughout the land of Canaan ever since the invasion led by Joshua, the only unity that they possessed was religious.

The stories of the Judges give examples of the struggles during the early days of settlement. A few adjacent tribes might join forces to break the power of a hostile tribe dominating them. Thus very slowly the territory regarded by the Jews as the Promised Land was claimed. But there was no longer one leader, such as Moses or Joshua, only chieftains or judges.

The coming of the Philistines from Crete to invade the land from the sea coast, at about the same time as the Hebrews were becoming established, presented a formidable threat. Nothing less than complete unity of all Hebrews under one leader would be sufficient to stop Philistine advance. (The name Palestine is derived from Philistine.)

The later editors of the Old Testament scriptures, looking back over centuries of monarchy, viewed it with mixed feelings. These feelings show in the history as we now have it (1 Samuel 8, 10[17-19]).

Many kings of both north and south had failed in giving spiritual leadership to their people, though often they were successful politically. Written into the narrative of the establishment of the monarchy, therefore, are the feelings of the editors who believed it to have been a mistake, and against the will of God, from the outset. In the earliest account of the choice of Saul as the first king, however (1 Samuel 9–10[1-16]), Samuel does not dispute the fact that the anointing of Saul was in accordance with the divine will. 'Has not the Lord anointed you to be prince over his people Israel?' (1 Samuel 10[1].)

The editors of the books of Samuel and Kings have one criterion only when estimating the reigns of the kings subsequent to the united monarchy. This was their attitude towards Baal worship. It did not matter how strong a king was in any other way; if he permitted, encouraged, or even was indifferent to, Baal worship, then in the eyes of the editors he 'did that which was evil in the sight of the Lord'.

A notable example of this attitude is that furnished by King Omri of Israel. He did much to establish and strengthen the Northern Kingdom. He built a capital city named Samaria, which even the Assyrians found hard to capture; he made a useful marriage alliance for his son, Ahab, to Jezebel, a princess from Tyre; and such was Omri's influence that the Assyrians long referred to Israel as Omri-land. Yet the book of Kings dismisses his achievements in twelve verses (1 Kings 16^{16-28}). Why?

Omri made no attempt to close the northern centres of worship at Dan and Bethel (condemned by the editors subsequent to the Deuteronomic Reform); and, being a king of the rival Northern Kingdom anyway, he did not stand a chance of favourable comment. Not only did he do 'what was evil in the sight of the Lord' but he 'did more evil than all who were before him' (1 Kings 16^{25}).

By contrast, Kings Hezekiah and Josiah of Judah tried to bring about some religious reforms, and so they 'did what was right in the eyes of the Lord' (2 Kings 18^{3}, 22^{2}).

This may seem to be a very harsh and biased way of judging the Hebrew monarchy. Such it undoubtedly was, but it is doubtful whether any completely unbiased history of anything has ever been written. The Hebrew editors were not concerned with writing a political success story. Israel never became a great world power: the chance for that was lost when David died. If the Hebrews had become political leaders it is unlikely that they could ever have been the spiritual leaders of mankind. Indeed their spiritual perception grew out of their struggles to hold their own against their enemies.

It is the spiritual, not the political, success story that concerns the editors. The Hebrews had been united by religion long before they had been united by politics. The worship of the Baals, with all their corruptions, threatened the religious unity of the nation, and, with it, its moral fibre. This then was the reason for the stern judgment of the editors. They knew that religion stemming from the covenant relationship with Yahweh was the source of the nation's strength, and the reason for its existence. If that were lost, then so too was all else.

It was not quite such a simple matter for the kings. Just as 'no man is an island', so no nation is one either. A nation cannot exist in isolation. It has contact with its neighbours for purposes of trade, and cannot exist without it. Good foreign relations also are essential for maintaining peace. This was the work and responsibility of the king, and, in ancient times, was closely associated with the religious beliefs of surrounding peoples.

David established around his kingdom a ring of friendly states. Solomon formed marriage alliances with foreign royalty. This sort of practice inevitably involved a king in foreign religions (though it also brought foreigners into covenant relationship with Yahweh). Treaties were made in the name of gods. Solomon made provision, even in the Temple itself, for the foreign cults followed by his various wives. Had it not been for the prophet Elijah, Ahab's marriage to Jezebel might have brought about the displacement of Yahweh worship in the north by the worship of Melkart, god of Tyre.

Some kings were much more conscious of such dangers than were others. These the editors commend. Only in the wilderness period had the Hebrews been free from contact with foreign religions.

The ideal of kingship

The Hebrew conception of kingship was both remarkable and unique. The oriental king could do exactly as he pleased; he was answerable to no one, and his people were subject to him for good or ill. In effect he was a despot. Not so the ideal Hebrew king: he was both the servant of God and of his people.

God was the real sovereign: the king was his vice-regent, and answerable to him. It was God's laws, and not his own, that the king was called upon to uphold. Both king and people were subject to those laws. Of course not every king lived up to this ideal all the time, but the fact that the ideal was held at all is surprising.

Two notable examples are given in the Old Testament of kings even being rebuked for violating the rights of one of their subjects.

The first concerns King David, who, wanting another man's wife, arranged for her husband to be killed in battle – and this, after David had unsuccessfully tried to make it appear that the husband was the father of the child whom Bathsheba was expecting. This brought about the stern rebuke of the prophet Nathan, which David accepted in the words: 'I have sinned against the Lord' (2 Samuel 11^2–12^{15}).

The second example comes from the Northern Kingdom of Israel. King Ahab wanted to extend his palace grounds, and wished to buy a vineyard from Naboth. Naboth did not wish to part with it. At first, Ahab was prepared to respect the rights of Naboth in the matter, but Queen Jezebel was accustomed to a different idea of kingship. If a king wanted, then he took. She took the affair in hand and arranged for

Naboth's death. The prophet Elijah denounced Ahab for permitting this (1 Kings 21).

Because the Hebrew king was God's representative, he had a dual role. He was expected to be both the political and the spiritual leader of his people, combining in his person the office of both king and priest. His coronation indicated the one, and his anointing by the chief religious personality of his day, the other. As king he could lead his armies into battle, make laws, hold supreme court, dispense justice. As priest he could lead his people in worship and offer sacrifice.

Thus David led his people in worship and rejoicing when the Ark was brought to Jerusalem, offering sacrifices and blessing the people in the name of the Lord of hosts (2 Samuel 6$^{12-19}$). King Solomon himself dedicated the Temple, and offered sacrifice (1 Kings 8). Relations between Samuel and Saul might not have been so strained had Samuel realized that the king had every right to offer sacrifice (1 Samuel 13$^{5-15}$).

The priestly role of the king is reflected in the Psalms. They are Israel's hymns for all occasions, and it is the king, the Lord's anointed, who is prominent in them. For example, Psalm 110 is a coronation anthem, and in it the king is told: 'You are a priest for ever after the order of Melchizedek'. Melchizedek was the early priest-king of Jerusalem mentioned in Genesis 14$^{17-20}$.

Melchizedek means 'king of righteousness' (just as the name of Zadok, the priest in 1 Kings 1, means 'righteousness'); and there is a strong connection between the name Melchizedek and the future Zadokites or Zedekites, later known as Sadducees. They were the aristocratic and very powerful priestly families in New Testament times. 'In the high-priesthood of Annas and Caiaphas '(Luke 3^2).

The dual role of priest and king seems to have been an impossible ideal for one man to fulfil. His work as king was more than enough to occupy him full time. This had to have priority. Someone else was needed to share this dual role and take some of the burden of spiritual leadership. Thus the king often worked in close alliance with a prophet, e.g. Saul with Samuel; David with Nathan; Ahab with Elijah; Ahaz and Hezekiah with Isaiah; Jehoiakim with Jeremiah.

The influence and intervention of the prophets was not always welcomed. Nevertheless an important feature of the work of the prophet was that of making up what was lacking in the king in the discharge of the priestly role.

The office of High Priest arose very late in Hebrew history, and was often equivalent to that of King. This was especially so of the Maccabaean or Hasmonaean rulers. They were high priests who called themselves kings, but this did not mean that the priestly role of a king was at last coming to the fore.

They could lead their people in worship, but, as with the kings of old, their interest and influence was political rather than spiritual. Their concern was to maintain good relations with any dominating foreign power. Political intrigue was more important than devotion to Yahweh. It was in these circumstances that the early Pharisees aimed to make up for the spiritual deficiency in the ruler (as the prophets had done in the past).

During the Seleucid rule of Palestine (198–64 B.C.) many strict and devout Jews resolved to resist the influence of foreign ideas. They saw their religion and priesthood corrupted, and so they were determined to remain true to their faith. Some even suffered martyrdom. They were known as the 'Pious Ones'. Later they became the party of 'Separated Ones' or Pharisees.

Whether the Hebrew head of state appears in a chronicle as King or High Priest, or both, he is always acting a dual role, but politics rather than religion is his first interest.

The Ideal King

The greatest of Hebrew kings was undoubtedly David. He established his kingdom, and brought peace and prosperity to it. During his reign its bounds were more extensive than ever again. David had the beginnings of an empire, Israel being surrounded by subject states and kingdoms whose rulers owed allegiance to him.

Nor was David's greatness in politics only. Had his successors continued his work, Israel might well have become one of the great world powers. As it was, David's son Solomon allowed Israel's territories to decrease, and introduced such hardship and taxation that, at his death, the kingdom split into north (Israel) and south (Judah) with only two tribes, Judah and Benjamin, remaining faithful to Solomon's son Rehoboam, not for his own sake, but out of high regard for his grandfather David.

The subsequent political history is one of struggles against neighbouring great powers, and of a country weakened by strife between the north and the south. The chance for political greatness had been lost. It is the greatest tribute to King David that the Hebrews longed and hoped for another king like him.

The more they suffered, the brighter grew the hope. It became much more than a mere looking back to a golden past. It was important to them that the royal succession should be kept in the family, or house, of David. This was not too difficult, since he was of the tribe of Judah, the strongest tribe, and the one mainly comprising the surviving southern kingdom.

This second David would be all that previous kings had failed to be.

He would be the Ideal King, the Anointed One (i.e. the Messiah in Hebrew, or the Christ in Greek). The prophet Isaiah referred to him as a 'shoot' or 'branch' growing from the root of Jesse (David's father). The Davidic line was, he thought, like a felled tree, but one out of whose stump new life would spring, new life for Israel.

Coupled with the hope of an Ideal King grew the thought of a day of judgment to precede his coming. It was called the 'day of the Lord'. The Hebrews hoped that God would not let them, his Chosen Covenant People, suffer for ever at the hands of their enemies. One day he would vindicate them and punish those enemies. Then the second David would reign in peace and prosperity, Israel would be great once more, and the whole world would look to her as the religious centre of all nations.

It was rather surprising for some Hebrews when prophets like Amos (and later John the Baptist) said that the coming judgment would fall not only upon wicked foreigners, but also upon any unfaithful Jews. Isaiah thought that only the faithful Israelites, a 'faithful remnant', would, after judgment, form the nucleus of the new Israel. Even so, the book of Isaiah particularly is full of glowing descriptions of the good time coming when all things would be wonderful. There would be complete harmony in the world of nature, and the wilderness would blossom as the crocus (Isaiah 35, 65^{25}).

The hopes concerning the Ideal King and the messianic age grew greater as prophets and poets pictured them in their imagination, and tried to describe something as yet unrealized. Many Hebrew writers indeed got quite carried away with their hopes and aspirations about the Messiah and the messianic age. At times it was obvious that no ordinary person could ever fulfil all their hopes, though some did so in part (e.g. Hezekiah, Jeremiah, Zerubbabel, and even King Cyrus of Persia).

It would be a mistake to think that even Jesus of Nazareth fulfilled all Messianic prophecy. At the beginning of his ministry he had to decide which of Israel's many hopes he was called upon to fulfil.

Care needs to be taken when considering Messianic prophecy. The Christian naturally works backward from the life of Jesus, and finds or selects all that is appropriate in the Old Testament. This was the method employed by the very first missionary teachers to the Jews. It is reflected in the Gospel according to St. Matthew. There Jesus of Nazareth is the promised Messiah. This or that incident in his life is said to fulfil certain words in the Scriptures, or, as the Gospel says, 'then was fulfilled what was spoken by the prophet' (e.g. Matthew 2^{17}). Sometimes the link between the Old Testament and the Gospel incident exists merely in the quotation of appropriate Old Testament words (Matthew 2$^{15, 17, 18}$). The student needs to look at messianic prophecy also from the standpoint of the Hebrews looking forward. Only in some instances do the two approaches correspond.

Isaiah's famous words to King Ahaz: 'Behold, a young woman [in the Authorized Version "a virgin"] shall conceive and bear a son, and shall call his name Immanuel' (Isaiah 7[14]), have tremendous significance for the Christian looking back upon them (as in Matthew 1[23]); but the words, when originally uttered by the prophet, indicated a sign which God would give to Ahaz in his own day. Isaiah was not consciously describing something which was to happen 700 years later.

Of all Palestinian cities, Micah might well choose Bethlehem as the one most appropriate for the birth of the Messiah; for it was King David's birthplace (Micah 5[2]; Matthew 2[6]). Jeremiah was not foretelling the massacre of the children of Bethlehem when he wrote, 'A voice is heard in Ramah, lamentation and bitter weeping' (Jeremiah 31[15]; Matthew 2[18]). Hosea was describing the Exodus from Egypt, not the return of Jesus, when he wrote, 'Out of Egypt I called my son' (Hosea 11[1]; Matthew 2[15]).

The words of Jeremiah and Hosea are quoted as appropriate comment in much the same way as we quote from Shakespeare.

Jesus himself probably fulfilled deliberately the words of Zechariah 9[9], when he demonstrated on Palm Sunday his claim to be the Messiah. In this connection it is interesting to note that the Gospel according to St. Matthew alone mentions two animals being brought to Jesus. This was a mistaken attempt on the part of the writer to make the event fit the prophecy more closely, the writer not realizing that the poetic repetition, 'a colt, the foal of an ass' (Matthew 21[5]), still means the same ass.

These examples do not mean that all so-called messianic prophecy is meaningless; far from it. But prophets were not crystal-gazers. It is in their hopes and aspirations, in the spirit of their writings, not in their exactitude, that fulfilment of their words can be found. This is where the divine inspiration was at work. This is the way in which Jesus made his own all that was noblest in the hopes of his people, and fulfilled them beyond the wildest prophetic dreams.

6. The Books of the Old Testament

Arrangement

The books of the Old Testament as printed are not arranged in sequence according to their date of writing. Genesis was not the first to be written, and is therefore not the oldest. Malachi, put last, is not the youngest. Many books are of complex authorship with the result that parts of a book are sometimes very old, and other parts much more recent (see p. 12).

The five Law books, i.e. the Pentateuch, are put together at the beginning of the Bible, for they comprise, for the Jew, the most important part of the Hebrew scripture. Most of the prophetic books are also grouped together, although not in an order corresponding to the lives of the prophets. These books, together with the historical books, make a group known as the Prophets. All books which are not part of the Law or the Prophets form a group known as the Writings. These are usually the youngest of the Old Testament books, and more predominantly works of literature. The historical books, and books containing a considerable amount of history, are arranged so as to form, as far as possible, a chronological account of the national history.

This grouping of the Old Testament books, according to their religious importance, into the Law, the Prophets, and the Writings, is of a general nature and does not mean that prophecy or laws are to be found only in their particular sections.

The Old Testament covers about 2000 years of Hebrew history and literature. This can roughly be divided into four sections, thus:

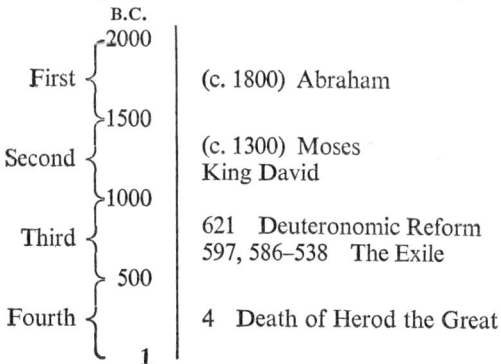

	B.C.	
First	⌐2000	(c. 1800) Abraham
	⊢1500	
Second		(c. 1300) Moses King David
	⊢1000	
Third		621 Deuteronomic Reform 597, 586–538 The Exile
	⊢ 500	
Fourth		4 Death of Herod the Great
	⌐ 1	

49

Most of the Old Testament books were compiled or edited, in the form in which we have them now, during the last of these sections of Hebrew history. They are therefore exilic or post-exilic in time of editing, but their contents may be dealing with a much earlier period of history, and contain much older material. The Deuteronomic Reform greatly affected the process of editing (see p. 8).

The Law

This is to be found in the first five books of the Old Testament, called collectively the Pentateuch. This, for the Jew, is (as we have seen) the most important part of the Scriptures. The books contain the sacred Law of Moses. Although all the laws were not written by him (e.g. Leviticus and Deuteronomy) they are written in the spirit of Moses, the first great Hebrew lawgiver (Exodus 24⁴).

The first great lawgiving took place at Mount Sinai while Moses was leading the people towards the Promised Land. The heart of Hebrew Law is the Decalogue, which is remarkable because of the equal emphasis that it puts upon religious and social obligations. Other laws were similar. There was no distinction between sacred and secular. This was a unique feature of Hebrew legislation, and a principle introduced right from the start.

Prophets constantly stressed the need for the two to grow together. Men like Amos pictured God as literally 'fed up' with costly sacrifices offered to him by people notorious for their social injustice. The observance of religious obligations alone would not satisfy God.

The Law books, Genesis, Exodus, and Numbers, contain also a substantial amount of Israel's early history, concerned with events leading up to the lawgiving at Sinai, and events following. Deuteronomy dates from the seventh century B.C., and Leviticus is probably exilic (see p. 13).

The Prophets

These writings rank second in importance to the Law in Jewish Scripture. Included in this section are the historical books of Samuel and Kings.

The prophets are referred to as major and minor, not on account of their importance as people, but because of the size of the books bearing their names. Thus Isaiah, Jeremiah and Ezekiel count as major prophets. The most important prophets for study are:

Eighth-century Prophets	⎧ Amos ⎪ Hosea ⎨ Isaiah of Jerusalem (Isaiah 1–39) ⎩ (Micah)
Last Days of Judah	Jeremiah
The Exile	⎰ Ezekiel ⎱ Deutero-Isaiah (Isaiah 40–55)
Post-exilic	⎧ Haggai ⎪ Zechariah 1–8 ⎪ Trito Isaiah (56–66) ⎨ Malachi ⎪ Joel ⎪ Ezra ⎩ Nehemiah

The most important function of the prophets up to the time of the Exile was that of reminding people of the covenant relationship with Yahweh. If they were not faithful to him, they could hardly expect him to stand by them in time of trouble – and the international situation usually seemed to indicate that trouble was not far away.

During the wanderings in the wilderness from Mount Sinai and the Covenant onwards, Hebrew religion was new and unchallenged. Upon entry into the Promised Land, however, the challenge came. A new land meant that the Hebrews were entering the territory of other gods – the Baals and the Ashtaroth (see p. 93). The worship of Yahweh soon became confused with Baal worship. It was the work of the prophets, not only to prevent this from happening, but also to teach that the Baals were useless and did not even exist.

Up to and during the Exile, the prophets made valuable contribution to man's knowledge of God, who was revealing himself to the Hebrews through them. Each prophet perceived some facet of God's character, and this dominated his religious ideas. The particular facet seen by a prophet was that which appealed most to his own character.

Amos was a stern man, and therefore saw the stern side of God's character, proclaiming his justice and righteousness. Hosea had domestic troubles and, through his own love and forgiveness for an unfaithful wife, came to know God's love and forgiveness for his sinful people. Isaiah was a man used to life at court in the presence of a king. It was therefore the holiness and majesty of God upon his throne that appealed most to him. Jeremiah saw the need for personal religion, and Deutero-Isaiah was the first to state that Yahweh was the one and only Creator.

The writings of the prophets give a very clear picture of the social conditions of their times. This is because they were not concerned with religion alone. They taught that religion must express itself in social behaviour. One might say that the prophets did not think of religion and politics as separate items. For them religion included politics.

The age of prophecy declined rapidly after the Exile. This was due to two factors: (*a*) The faithful Jews returning from the Exile were no longer tempted towards Baal worship: Yahweh alone was God. (*b*) During the Exile much work had been done by priests and other editors in compiling Hebrew Law. The Law was now there to guide people, and the new non-sacrificial type of service (later synagogue service) devised during the Exile was specially intended to make the Law known and understood by everyone.

Nothing has yet been said here about prophets foretelling the future (see p. 36). This was far from being their main function. It is often said that they were 'forth-tellers' not 'foretellers', that is that they were outspoken on important issues, rather than men who made predictions. In general, where predicting the future was involved, they were concerned with the immediate future. Most lived at times of great international unrest, and could see more clearly than others that certain courses of action taken by their nation would lead to disaster. They believed that God would permit such disaster if people were complacent regarding him, and were content to rely upon help from other nations. This caused the prophets to be so outspoken in the name of God.

Sometimes their hopes for the future took them further ahead, as when they declared that God would not always let his people suffer, that one day he would vindicate them, and bring judgment upon their enemies and his. There would come the Ideal Ruler, the second David, to rule over them in peace and prosperity as God's vice-regent, his Messiah, or Anointed One.

The more they thought of this, the more they were carried away with their ideas. They foretold the future as they hoped and believed that it would be, but it was not until Christian times that their words acquired a true significance, and one, of course, largely, if not entirely, unknown to them. Thus their specific predictions belonged to their own time, but their more distant hopes and speculations belong to the ages following.

Since they could not be more definite about this more distant future, some prophets employed the particular style of writing called apocalyptic (see p. 58).

The Writings

This is the third section of Hebrew Scripture. It comprises all books that do not fall into the categories of the Law and the Prophets. Since the Old Testament is a collection of a considerable amount of Hebrew history and literature, it is the literary works which form the Writings. Some of these works of literature have more religious value than others, notably the books of Psalms; and also Job, which probes the difficult problem of innocent suffering. There was some hesitation about including with them as Scripture the books Esther and the Song of Solomon, because the spiritual content of these compositions was not obvious.

The Law had been accepted as canonical or official Scripture from the time of the Exile. The Prophets came to be so regarded some time later. But the decision as to what other Hebrew literature might be worthy of inclusion was not taken until the Council of Rabbis at Jamnia in about A.D. 100. Eleven books were selected. These books became the Writings.

The Apocrypha

The original language of the Old Testament was Hebrew, but some time around the third century B.C. the Jewish community at Alexandria began work on translating the Hebrew Scriptures into Greek, the language of their daily speech. How long this took is not known. There were by now Jews dispersed throughout the Roman Empire whose connection with Palestine was very slight. Even in Jerusalem there was a synagogue for Jews speaking Greek.

The Greek translation, known as the Septuagint (often written LXX) from the Latin for seventy, and so called from a legend that it was the work of seventy scholars, included a further fourteen books in addition to the Law, the Prophets and the Writings. The Council of Jamnia did not approve of them, and they were excluded from the official Hebrew Scriptures. The fourteen extra books contained in the Septuagint, but so excluded, are known as the Apocrypha.

Apocrypha is from a Greek word meaning hidden. The fourteen books were 'hidden' in the sense that they were suppressed or banned for devout Hebrew-speaking Jews, as opposed to the Greek-speaking Jews who used the Septuagint.

The Septuagint version of the Old Testament was much used by the early Christians, few of whom, even in Palestine, would have been able to read Hebrew.

The Apocrypha, with the rest of the Septuagint, was translated into the Latin version, the Vulgate, meaning the common version. It is regarded in the Roman Catholic Church as canonical, i.e. Scripture complying with the standard or rule of the Church. Other Christians do not regard the Apocrypha as so authoritative, but many value it as a useful supplement. It is available both separately and as an integral part of the Authorized and Revised Versions, the American Revised Standard Version and the New English Bible.

THE LAW
The Pentateuch: Genesis, Exodus, Leviticus, Numbers, Deuteronomy

THE PROPHETS
The former prophets: Joshua, Judges, Samuel, Kings
The latter prophets: Isaiah, Jeremiah, Ezekiel
The twelve minor prophets: Hosea, Joel, Amos, Obadiah, Jonah, Micah, Nahum, Habakkuk, Zephaniah, Haggai, Zechariah, Malachi

THE WRITINGS
Job, Psalms, Proverbs
The Five Rolls: Ruth, Esther, Ecclesiastes, Song of Solomon, Lamentations
Chronicles, Ezra, Nehemiah, Daniel

THE APOCRYPHA
1 Esdras, 2 Esdras, Tobit, Judith, Additions to Esther, The Wisdom of Solomon, Ecclesiasticus, Baruch and the Letter of Jeremiah, The Song of the Three Young Men, Susanna, Bel and the Dragon, The Prayer of Manasseh, 1 Maccabees, 2 Maccabees

Wisdom Literature

Three books of the Old Testament are classed as Wisdom Literature: Job, Proverbs, and Ecclesiastes. Two more in this category, the Wisdom of Solomon and Ecclesiasticus, are found in the Apocrypha. These books belong to the late period of Hebrew history following the Greek invasion by Alexander the Great in 331 B.C.

It was not unusual for primitive communities to have a 'wise man' or 'wise woman' whose advice could be sought. Usually such people were old: they had acquired their wisdom over the years, and long experience had made them wise. Frequently they claimed to add to their wisdom by resorting to mysterious aids, beyond the understanding of the layman. Such wise men and wise women are more often referred to as wizards and witches. The Deuteronomic Reform banned the practice of this kind of wisdom, so closely allied to magic, among the Hebrews (2 Kings 23^{24}).

Saul and his servant, in search for lost asses, went to consult Samuel, whom Saul referred to as a seer. Samuel was a wise man who could be described as a 'man of God'. He predicted future events for Saul, and assured him of the safety of the animals. Thus Samuel possessed a knowledge beyond that of the ordinary man (1 Samuel 9). So too, it appeared, did the people who presided at oracles (Judges 4^5); and Joseph, the interpreter of dreams (Genesis 41^{39}).

Wisdom, in the form of intelligence, quick wit, and shrewdness, was ascribed to Solomon — hence the complimentary title of the book in the

Apocrypha. Wisdom was an invaluable asset to a king, who was also chief judge in his kingdom. The story of the two harlots and the baby, not unlike stories told of other rulers, was meant to illustrate this gift. The later Wisdom 'school' of thinkers and writers often made Solomon the focal point of their more advanced conception of wisdom.

They came to see wisdom as the most sought after of God's gifts bestowed upon man. Thus Solomon is said to have pleased God by asking for this gift rather than for any other (1 Kings 3$^{5-14}$). Yet wisdom, in the simple form of foresight, might have saved him from the short-sighted policy which led to the division of his kingdom at his death.

Wise, meaning learned, was another connotation of the idea of wisdom. The 'wise' man was one whose learning, sacred or secular, gave him knowledge beyond that of the ordinary man. Jeremiah had cause to denounce the complacent advice that such wise men gave to a nation on the brink of exile. 'How can you say, "We are wise, and the law of the Lord is with us"? But, behold, the false pen of the scribes has made it into a lie. The wise men shall be put to shame . . . they have rejected the word of the Lord, and what wisdom is in them?' (Jeremiah 8^8, ^{9}.) The intellectual leaders of the nation were leading it to disaster, and their 'wisdom' was unable to see it.

Much of the Wisdom Literature consists of good advice to the man who wanted to live a moral life. After the Exile particular emphasis was laid upon making the Law applicable and intelligible to the individual. The Wisdom writers helped in this by stressing the desirability of acquiring wisdom (Proverbs 8^{11}; Wisdom 7^9).

The highest conception of wisdom reached was that of Divine Wisdom, not merely as God's gift of intelligence to men who sought it, but the wisdom which is a facet, almost a consort, of God himself: 'the wisdom that sits by thy throne' (Wisdom 9^4). This was the most to be desired of all.

The idea of the Divine Wisdom grew out of a consideration of the relationship between God and his world. People who believed in God, whether Jews or Gentiles, thought deeply about this. The divine Being must, as it were, be apart from the world; and yet there was evidence of divine activity within the world, giving and sustaining life. Divine reason and intelligence were obviously at work giving purpose to creation (Wisdom 9^2; Ecclesiasticus 24^3).

In Hebrew thought the link between God and the world, or the extension of God within the world, was variously referred to as the Word (*dabar*), the Glory (*shechinah*), the Spirit (*ruach*), the Wisdom (*hokmah*) of God. When the divine Being, apart from the world, spoke, the divine will was accomplished within the world. God's Word was therefore something divine in itself, proceeding from God, and bringing

55

the divine purpose, reason, and intelligence, actively into the world. The term Word of God is very frequently used in the Old Testament and the Apocrypha to express this thought.

Perhaps the most notable example is in the Creation parable in Genesis 1, with its repetition: 'And God said . . . and it was so'. The Word of God was thus the means by which God created the world. Likewise in the Psalms the same thought is expressed: 'By the word of the Lord the heavens were made, and all their host by the breath of his mouth'; 'For he spoke, and it came to be; he commanded, and it stood forth' (Psalm 33 6, 9).

The writings of Deutero-Isaiah well convey the idea of the continuous activity of the Word of God in the world. 'So shall my word be that goes forth from my mouth; it shall not return to me empty, but it shall accomplish that which I purpose, and prosper in the thing for which I sent it' (Isaiah 55 11).

The Word of God was also the means by which he communicated with men. The prophets in particular were regarded as the mouthpieces of God, and it was his word that they uttered. Thus Jeremiah could say: 'Now the word of the Lord came to me saying'; 'Then the Lord put forth his hand and touched my mouth; and the Lord said to me, "Behold, I have put my words in your mouth." ' (Jeremiah 1 4, 9.) (Cf. Hosea 1 1 Jonah 1 1, Micah 1 1, Zephaniah 1 1.)

Similarly the Glory (*shechinah*, meaning 'that which dwells') of God was an indication of the divine presence in the world. Moses said: 'I pray thee show me thy glory' (Exodus 33 18); 'The glory of the Lord filled the tabernacle' (Exodus 40 34–38). The seraphim of Isaiah's vision proclaimed that 'the whole earth is full of his glory' (Isaiah 6 3). Deutero-Isaiah prophesied: 'And the glory of the Lord shall be revealed' (Isaiah 40 5). The psalmist wrote: 'The heavens are telling the glory of God' (Psalm 19 1). (Cf. Leviticus 9 23; Numbers 14 22, 16 42; 1 Kings 8 10, 11; Ezekiel 1 28, 3 23, 10 4; Haggai 2 7.)

The Spirit of God was a term used in the same way. At the Creation, 'the Spirit of God was moving over the face of the waters' (Genesis 1 2). It, too, denoted the divine activity continually at work. 'When thou sendest forth thy Spirit, they are created; and thou renewest the face of the ground' (Psalm 104 30). Another psalmist prayed: 'Cast me not away from thy presence, and take not thy holy Spirit from me' (Psalm 51 11).

The opening words of the first Servant Song says of God's servant: 'I have put my Spirit upon him' (Isaiah 42 1). Referring to these same Servant Songs another prophet commented: 'The Spirit of the Lord God is upon me, because the Lord has anointed me to bring good tidings to the afflicted' (Isaiah 61 1).

The Hebrew word for spirit is *ruach*, and it means wind or breath. Thus the breath of God, like his word, proceeds from him, and the wind is a symbol of his energy and activity. Ezekiel, in his vision of the valley of dry bones, realized that by the Spirit of God a nation dead in Exile could live again. 'And I will put my Spirit within you, and you shall live' (Ezekiel 37[14]). (Cf. Judges 3[10], 6[34], 13[25]; 1 Samuel 10[5, 6]; Psalm 139[7]; Isaiah 40[13], 44[3], 63[10-14]; Ezekiel 11[1]; Joel 2[28]; Zechariah 4[6].)

While Hebrew theology was using the terms Word, Glory and Spirit to denote the link between God and the world, the Greeks also were feeling after a similar idea. As early as 600 B.C. the philosopher Heraclitus used the term *logos* (Greek for 'word') to describe the relation between the eternal world and this physical world. The term stressed the idea of a divine reason or principle, which holds the universe together and gives unity to it, both in nature and in the human soul. The use of the term *logos* had much less significance than the Hebrew term *dabar*; for, whereas the Jews firmly believed in one God and Creator, who was deliberately revealing himself to man and communicating with man, Greek thinkers by no means all believed in one God or Supreme Being.

From 331 B.C. many of the lands bordering the Mediterranean became part of the Greek Empire, due to the conquests of Alexander the Great. Greek thought and culture became fashionable, and the Greek language almost international. Many Jews lived in countries other than Palestine, and in Alexandria (Alexander's memorial city) there was a strong Jewish colony. Such Jews were much in touch with Greek thought, and it was here that the Jewish philosopher Philo, familiar with both Greek thought and Hebrew theology, combined the Greek *logos* and the Hebrew *dabar* into a single concept. Later Jewish–Greek writing reflected this double influence.

The Wisdom (*hokmah*, or in Greek *sophia*) of God inspired the latest development of Hebrew theology. The idea flourished during the Greek period, giving rise to the Wisdom Literature. The term was used along with or in place of the Word, e.g. 'Who hast made all things by thy word, and by thy wisdom hast formed man' (Wisdom 9[1]).

In a way the term Wisdom conveyed more depth of meaning than Word, for Divine Wisdom suggests much more the reason and intelligence existing in the mind of a personal God. People think, then speak and act – thought, word, and deed. In similar fashion God's wisdom, God's word, and God's activity in the world indicate belief in a personal divine being.

As the idea develops in the Old Testament and the Apocrypha, the Word or Wisdom of God tends to become distinct from God, and to possess an existence of its own, although still God, until Wisdom is almost personified and referred to as 'she'. The Divine Wisdom, like the Word, was not only the Creator of the world but was also the quality most sought after by men: 'When he marked out the foundation of the earth, then I was beside him, like a master workman' (Proverbs 8[29, 30]); 'Give me the wisdom that sits by thy throne' (Wisdom 9[4]); 'Because all gold is but a little sand in her sight' (Wisdom 7[9]); 'For wisdom is better than jewels' (Proverbs 8[11]).

The idea of the Divine Wisdom is perhaps best summed up in the following quotation, which also suggests something of the Spirit and the Glory of God: 'She is a breath of the power of God, and a pure emanation of the glory of the Almighty. . . . For she is a reflection of eternal light, a spotless mirror of the working of God, and an image of his goodness' (Wisdom 7[25, 26]). (Cf. Job 28[12-28]; Proverbs 8[22-31], 9[10]; Wisdom 7[7, 22], 8[1-5], 9[1-4, 9-11, 17], 18[14, 15]; Ecclesiasticus 1[1-20], 24[3, 9-12, 19-21], 51[23, 26]; Matthew 11[28-30]; John 1[1-3, 14], 6[35]; 1 Corinthians 1[24].)

Apocalyptic Writing

The Hebrew nation, weak in relation to its neighbours, was always suffering at the hands of enemies. More often than not it had a real struggle for survival, as it came under the domination of one major power after another: Assyria, Babylon, Egypt, Greece, Rome. The breakaway Northern Kingdom of Israel got lost in the struggle, and the Southern Kingdom of Judah was threatened with extinction.

Despite such formidable odds the Hebrew people did survive. So too did the belief that they were chosen by God for a special purpose, and that surely some day he would vindicate their sufferings. This thought sustained them. They looked for a day of judgment, when their enemies and Yahweh's would be punished. At the judgment, a Messiah would preside as God's vice-regent, and afterwards a new age would dawn for faithful Israel.

Many prophets tried to make people realize that this 'day of the Lord' would not bring judgment exclusively upon foreign nations, as some fondly hoped, but upon Israel's own wrong-doers also. Thus Amos said to the self-satisfied, 'Why would you have the day of the Lord? It is darkness, and not light' (Amos 5[18]).

The same unpopular truth was still being preached by the last of the prophets, John the Baptist, as he told his hearers, 'Do not begin to say to yourselves, "We have Abraham as our father" ', i.e. 'We are Jews' (Luke 3[8]).

The prophet Isaiah believed that after the judgment the faithful remnant of Israel would form the nucleus of a new nation, ruled over by a descendant of David. Isaiah likened the nucleus to a new shoot growing out of the stump of a felled tree (Isaiah 11[1, 10]).

Speculation grew about the nature of the day of the Lord, and writers tried to describe it. But they were attempting to describe something yet to occur. It would be unique, so it could not easily be compared with anything already known. Therefore a special style of writing came to be developed, called apocalyptic. The name implies an uncovering or unveiling of future events. In apocalyptic literature such events were often described in the form of visions, in which symbolic language was used rather than plain speech or even poetry. A vocabulary of such symbolism came into being.

People were encouraged to endure their present sufferings. These were to be regarded as a necessary prelude to the day of the Lord, when the power of good would overcome the power of evil. Before this happened, however, there would be a final outburst of evil, when all that was opposed to God would do its worst. This anti-God element in apocalyptic thought was sometimes symbolized by a dragon or beast.

It was also thought that nature too would react with catastrophes and supernatural signs. The sun and the moon would not give light, and the stars would fall (Isaiah 13$^{9-11}$, 24$^{21-23}$; Ezekiel 32$^{7-10}$; Joel 2$^{30-32}$). Later on Jesus used this conventional type of language when speaking of the future destruction of Jerusalem (in A.D. 70), and of his second coming (Mark 13$^{24-27}$).

This style of writing therefore became popular with Christians, who adopted some of the symbolic vocabulary. The day of the Lord became for them the second coming of Jesus. Before this second advent, evil or anti-Christ would have its final outburst in the form of wars, famines, and the persecution of Christians. As in the Jewish apocalyptic writings, these sufferings were to be seen as the prelude to God's final triumph over the powers of evil. Thus the faithful were encouraged to remain steadfast.

The Gospels contain much apocalyptic material, notably Mark 13, and the passages in Matthew and Luke based upon it (Matthew 24; Luke 17$^{22-37}$, 21$^{5-38}$). A number of the parables acquired apocalyptic emphasis when used by the first Christians, who were expecting an early second advent of Christ. All the parables involving a selection process of good from bad, worthy from unworthy, ready from unready, have been seen as illustrations of the day of judgment. Some have been recorded with this emphasis, e.g. the Tares (Matthew 13$^{24-30, 36-43}$), the Dragnet (Matthew 13$^{47-50}$).

A banquet, and particularly a marriage feast, was a commonly recognized symbol for the Messianic kingdom, and a bridegroom was symbolic of the Messiah.

The great parable of the Judgment, the Sheep and the Goats (Matthew 25$^{31-46}$), is more of an apocalypse than a parable. An apocalypse is a complete book, or section of a book, in this style of writing. For this reason the last book of the Bible is called the Apocalypse, or the Revelation (the corresponding word in Latin); and Mark 13 is often referred to as the Little Apocalypse.

Many books of the Bible contain examples of apocalyptic writing, e.g. Isaiah 25–27, Daniel 7–12, Zechariah 9–14. Apocalyptic writing possesses a distinct literary style which a student should try to recognize; for it would be a mistake to suppose that apocalyptic authors were giving factual information or accurate descriptions of future events. Their language, like that of a poet, was a means of conveying a message beyond the scope of actual word pictures.

7. Stories with Special Meanings

The compilers of the Old Testament library included a number of stories whose spiritual or moral value lies in the author's particular message, and not in the actuality of the incidents portrayed. The parables of Jesus in the New Testament are perhaps the best known and the simplest examples of this kind of story.

The fact that parable and allegory are used also by Old Testament authors is sometimes overlooked. Some of these parables and allegories exist in the Old Testament as separate books, e.g. Jonah (see p. 69). Others are incorporated in larger compilations.

An important group of parables and allegories occurs at the beginning of the book of Genesis. The book of Genesis, as its name implies, is a book of origins. Hebrew national history begins with Moses and the Exodus from Egypt. The book of Genesis forms a prologue to such national history, showing God as shaping the course of events leading up to the Exodus.

The prologue is twofold – historical and theological. The historical prologue begins with the call of Abraham in Genesis 12, the origin of the Chosen People. The theological prologue is to be found in the parables of Creation, the Fall, the Tower of Babel, and the Flood. These parables try to answer theologically the question: Why should God select Abraham, Isaac, and Jacob for a special purpose?

The answer that the parables suggest is that God made the universe, and that what he made was good; but that the perfection of his creation, and especially the relationship of man with God, was marred by human disobedience, pride, and jealousy. God, however, being merciful, gave man a fresh start, a second chance as it were, and himself again took the initiative. Some of the myths and legends of ancient Greece and Rome, though spiritually inferior to the Hebrew compilations, were the result of similar attempts to answer theologically questions concerning man arising from his environment.

The compilers of the Old Testament did well to include these particular parables, for they introduce the divine drama of redemption on to the stage of human history.

Who made the world? (Genesis 1–2³: source P)

This wonderful literary work belongs to some unknown priestly writer of the Exile (586–538 B.C.). The Exile in Babylon had brought home to the Hebrews the realization that God was the supreme Creator of all the Universe. The prophet of the Exile whose writings are to be found in Isaiah 40–55 had stated this truth in no uncertain way (Isaiah 44⁶, ⁸). It was the great theological advance of that period. Before this realization, the Hebrews had been polytheistic like other neighbouring tribes, although there were always some, like Moses himself, who were monotheist in the sense that only Yahweh mattered.

Now, in a masterpiece of literature, someone unknown tried to enshrine the truth that God is the Creator, that what he made was good, and that man was the crown of his creation.

The majesty and dignity of the Creator is presented in truly magnificent fashion as he calls each stage of creation into being. The writer could have described all creation collectively, as one great creative act of God. How much more dramatic, though, is the stage by stage creation, emphasizing over and over again that a purposeful God is the source of all that is! The words 'And God said, Let there be . . .' are repeated like a refrain. The idea of God's Word being in itself creative and active, and his means of communication with this world, runs throughout the Old Testament (see p. 56). Also like a refrain comes the insistence that God's creation is good. It is possible that this parable was a creation hymn used liturgically in the Temple.

The writer carefully arranged the stages of creation to fit the six-day working week of his own time. The seventh day was widely observed as a day of rest, and had been so for centuries. People needed a regular day off from work, and this was the reason given to the Hebrews in the earliest edition of the Ten Commandments (Exodus 34²¹). God was therefore given his working week and day off, for this was the pattern of life. (From this point of view a twentieth-century writer could possibly give him a weekend, or even have him work overtime!)

So successful was this parable of Creation that it was used to give added sanctity to the Sabbath, and mention of it was added to the later Ten Commandments (Exodus 20¹¹).

Many peoples of the world have their myths regarding their origin, and not least the people of Babylon with whom the Hebrews had a double contact, both through Abraham, who came from Ur, and through the Exile. Their 'Epic of Creation', a poem dating from the time of Abraham, describes how their god Marduk destroyed a monster of the deep named Tiamat. Half the monster's body became the heaven and half became the earth.

Students will in fact find a number of points of similarity between the Babylonian myth and the biblical parable. This is not surprising in view of the Hebrew links with Babylon. In any age the majority of writers are influenced by what others have written previously. It is in its points of difference that the biblical parable rises so far above the Babylonian myth (see *Ancient Near Eastern Texts*).

Why is there sin and suffering? (Genesis 2⁴–3: source J)

The parable of the Fall is the Hebrew attempt to answer this question. It teaches that disobedience to the will of God was the cause of human sin and suffering. It did not come from God, for his creation was good. Man brought it upon himself.

The story shows a great insight into human nature, even though it was written nearly 3000 years ago. Mr. and Mrs. Everyman, or, in Hebrew, Adam (i.e. man) and Eve (i.e. life) are placed by God in the beautiful Garden of Eden. (The writer may have had the land of Babylon in mind.) This was to emphasize the perfection that God wanted for man.

As the crown of creation, man names the animals. Thus the writer indicates man's dominion over them. The fact that man is essentially a social being is seen in the reason for the creation of woman; the close ties between male and female are shown in the creation of woman from man.

Everything in the garden, or rather in the world, was therefore beautiful, until the perfection of creation was spoilt by sin. All sin is, in some way, that which is contrary to the known law of God. So it was appropriate that the writer of this story used an act of disobedience to symbolize mankind's downfall.

It is interesting too that in the serpent he saw evil as an external force, acting upon mankind from outside, and not as something coming from within.

The tree was the 'tree of the knowledge of good and evil'. (There is no mention in the text of apples!) Until there was sin, there could be no realization that there could be any knowledge other than of what is good, or that the result of sin is death. Eve was deceived by the outward appearance of the 'fruit', and reason seemed to tell her that it would benefit both herself and her husband (cf. the temptations of Jesus, where they also appeared reasonable).

It was not a sin committed in ignorance, for God had made his will clear to them both. In a sense it was a sin of thinking that they knew better. How true to human experience it is that what is forbidden has a peculiar fascination: it presents a challenge.

A sense of guilt, symbolized by the awareness that they were naked, quickly followed the act of disobedience. The feeling of shame made them try to hide, not only from each other, but from God. A barrier of sin had come between man and God, and their once happy relationship was marred. Fear of meeting God is the reaction of the sinner.

In the parable Adam and Eve behave rather like two school-children in the presence of the headmaster, giving themselves away even before they are questioned. Then comes the very human shifting of the blame: the man blames the woman 'whom thou gavest to be with me', therefore in a way blaming God himself; the woman blames the serpent.

Human toil, strife, pain and death were seen by the writer as the inevitable result of man's fall. Man was no longer fit to dwell in the presence of God; he was barred from it, and there was no turning back.

It is quite remarkable how much understanding and insight the writer has packed into every word of this superb parable. It would be difficult to write a better one. It forms a very worthy introduction to the Bible library, for it gives the theological reason for the necessity of a divine plan of redemption. It is, after all, the main theme of the Bible: man has fallen, and God takes the initiative – through a Chosen People to whom he reveals himself, and through Christ's victory over evil – to restore the relationship between himself and mankind.

It is for this reason that Jesus is sometimes referred to as the second Adam (e.g. by St. Paul in 1 Corinthians $15^{20-22, 45}$). Jesus' favourite title for himself was Son of Man, i.e. Ben-Adam. The first Adam represented sinful mankind, bringing death upon the human race. Christ by his resurrection brought the hope of life to all who belong to him. His obedience to God reversed Adam's disobedience.

The writer of the parable himself gave a faint hint of the hope of man's ultimate victory over evil when he spoke of the seed of the woman as bruising the serpent's head (Genesis 3^{15}). It has naturally followed that Christians have seen how appropriately these words may be applied to Jesus.

The story of Cain and Abel (Genesis 4: source J) forms a sequel to that of the Fall. Disobedience to God had brought sin to mankind, represented by Adam and Eve's sons. So the Fall is seen to be hereditary (producing what theologians call original sin). Future generations suffer the consequences. This second story shows jealousy and murder within a family to be one of those consequences.

We may compare the parable of the Fall with the Greek myth of Pandora's Box, wherein disobedience to a divine command is seen as the cause of mankind's ills. It is interesting to note that both in Greek myth and Hebrew parable it is the female who is guilty, though in the Hebrew story the man shares the guilt.

It is also interesting to compare the theology of the parables of the Creation and the Fall with the beliefs concerning creation current in the

Gnostic sects of the first centuries A.D. Whereas the Hebrew parables teach that God's creation was good, and that Man's sin spoilt it, the Gnostic sects came to terms with the idea of evil in the material world in a different way.

For them God was good, but he delegated his work of creation to a series of creating angels, each one more removed from himself. The last in the series of the creating angels was the sub-contractor responsible for the creation of the world. This myth dealt with the problem of any direct or personal contact between the good creator and a world which contained evil.

Those Gnostic sects which incorporated a little so-called Christianity into their systems looked upon Jesus as the creating angel nearest to God, and the God of the Old Testament as the angel responsible for the creation of the world.

Why different languages? (Genesis 11$^{1-9}$: source J)

The writer of the Tower of Babel parable has based it upon historical events. The historical basis is the building of the city of Babylon in the land of Chaldaea or Shinar. So important did the city become that the land around it became known as Babylonia.

A focal point of an ancient city was its temple. In Babylonia such temples were often built on the top of artificially constructed mountains of considerable height. Known as ziggurats, the structures rose in a series of terraces and gardens to the temple on the summit. Such constructions dominated a city, and in the flat country around served as landmarks for miles. Some probably had the name of a city inscribed upon them. Ancient inscriptions concerning these ziggurats sometimes indicate the desire that they should reach the heavens, of which the visible sky was thought to be the floor.

Archaeologists have tried to identify, from the remains of many ziggurats, the actual one which the writer of the Tower of Babel story had in mind. Many suggestions have been made, but the two most favoured are the ziggurats known as the Birs Nimrud, the ruins of which are 150 feet high, and the E-temenanki, or Temple of E-Sagila (meaning reaching to the clouds). This latter is now thought to be the more likely, for the ruins lie within the walls of the ancient city of Babylon. The E-temenanki was so high, according to various records, that its top was often in need of repair, and it is recorded that Nebuchadnezzar, responsible for one such repair, said that the summit of the tower rivalled the heavens.

The author of the story has given added force to it by a clever play upon words. The English name Babylon comes from the Greek name

Babulon and means 'Gate of God'. The English name Babel comes from *Babilu*, the Hebrew equivalent of Babylon, but the writer has substituted a similar Hebrew word, *balal*, meaning 'to confuse', to draw out the point of his parable (see R.S.V. margin). Thus the attempt to build a tower which should have been Babel, the Gate of God, ended in *balal*, confusion.

The simple moral of the parable is that human pride (symbolized by Babylonian aggrandizement) is the cause of world disunity. Different languages are a reminder of this disunity.

It might at first appear that God was displeased by human achievement. This, however, is not the reason for God's displeasure. There is still more depth to the story. The rise of a heathen world power such as Babylon was, for the Jews, not only an apt illustration of human pride, but also an illustration of secularism. In the eyes of the Jews, Babylon was a proud and godless city and for them came to represent any other nation whose pride and achievement caused it ever to seek more power and dominion. The author of the book of Revelation used the name Babylon in this way, when pronouncing judgment on Imperial Rome.

It is not therefore ordinary natural human pride in achievement which caused God to act in this parable, but a godless desire for power carried too far. This sort of pride knows no limits.

In the parable, the Tower of Babel is designed to have 'its top in the heavens'. In the days when the visible sky was thought to be the floor of heaven, an attempt to build such a tower was presumption indeed. It indicated a desire for equality with God, or, worse still, the displacement of God. In modern times this attitude is well expressed in the last lines of Swinburne's *Hymn to Man*: 'Glory to Man in the highest! For Man is the master of things.'

The parable thus gives more than an explanation for different languages: it gives a warning to those who would displace God by their technology.

The New Testament gives a sequel to the Tower of Babel parable. In the story of the coming of the Holy Spirit upon the disciples at the time of the feast of Pentecost, people of 'every nation under heaven' understood what was said by the disciples. Christian theologians have long seen profound significance in this phenomenon. The disunity and confused language in the Tower of Babel is reversed by a new unity in Christ through the power of the Holy Spirit (Acts 2^{1-12}).

Why are there natural disasters? (Genesis 6–9: sources J and P)

This is a question which, even in the twentieth century, it is still hard to answer satisfactorily. After any disaster the question 'Why?' comes to the minds of most people. Sometimes the immediate answer can be found in human ignorance or negligence, but not always. Then one has to probe further.

Floods are common among the natural disasters of this country and of many others. Often they cannot be foreseen, and come as a complete surprise for the first time in history. This was so with the floods in Florence in 1966. Floods involve the loss of homes, possessions, animals and human life, and sometimes extend for hundreds of square miles.

The land of Mesopotamia, the low-lying land between the rivers Tigris and Euphrates, at the northern end of the Persian Gulf, was, so tradition and archaeology say, much subject to flooding. It was the scene of a particularly extensive flood in about 3000 B.C., involving great loss of life. The location was then known as Sumeria, and later as Babylonia. By the time of Abraham the great flood was already legendary.

Its story survives in Sumerian literature, in Babylonian literature in the Epic of Gilgamesh, and in Hebrew literature in the story of Noah. The Babylonian name for Noah's counterpart was Ut-napishtim. Both Abraham's stay in Babylonia, and the Hebrew exile there, left strong Babylonian influence on Hebrew tradition.

The biblical story of Noah in its present form is the work of a Hebrew editor of about 500 B.C. He has combined two earlier Hebrew versions, one dating from the ninth century B.C. (source J) and one much more recent, compiled by Hebrew priests exiled in Babylon in about 500 B.C. (source P). The priestly version was based on the older version and traditions. According to the priestly version, Noah took one pair of every animal into the ark, but according to the older version it was seven pairs, except of unclean beasts (Genesis 6[19], 7[2]).

A student could well make a detailed study of the significant variations in the Hebrew versions, and of their similarities with the Sumerian and Babylonian accounts of the Flood; but, as with the other Genesis parables that owe something of their imagery to Babylon, it is the differences which are the more important. It is the way in which Hebrew theologians altered, sometimes drastically, the Babylonian originals, that gives us an insight into Hebrew religion. By comparison with the Hebrew parables, the Babylonian originals have no theological value whatsoever, and the similarity is due to no more than literary influence (see *Ancient Near Eastern Texts*).

As a parable, the story of Noah, based upon an actual flood, has a message. In answer to the question 'Why are there natural disasters?'

the Hebrews usually had the answer that such were God's punishment for sin. In this parable, accordingly, the wicked are killed and the righteous Noah and his family are spared. This corresponds to the Hebrew belief that a long life was God's reward for the righteous, since, until much later, there was no belief in an after-life. The writer used what must have seemed to be a world-wide flood as a warning that sin could make God regret having created man.

The parable, coming in the Bible after that of the Fall and the first murder, presents the idea of God as making a fresh start with his creation. This idea is important theologically. At the end of the parable, God is seen making a covenant of mercy with Noah and with all mankind (symbolized by the rainbow). It is as though God were resigned to the sinfulness of mankind, and his anger is turned to mercy. He is about to put into operation his own plan of redemption, by calling Abraham to form his Chosen People (Genesis 12).

Ruth

This story is based upon some primitive pastoral happening, but the author or editor had a particular purpose in making use of it. The story is set in the time of the Judges, but he presumably lived centuries later, after the Exile in Babylon. Apparently he made use of some very ancient traditions regarding Ruth in order to protest against the stern attitude of some post-exilic leaders, especially Ezra, towards the matter of mixed marriages between Jews and Gentiles.

During the Exile the Jewish community would not have remained distinct in Babylon, had an exclusive policy towards foreigners not been adopted. The returning exiles, however, continued this policy after their return. Existing mixed marriages were closely examined, and became subject to annulment. These were drastic measures, but inspired no doubt by the fear that contact with Gentiles might once again tempt some Hebrews to foreign forms of worship.

The writer of Ruth points out that the Hebrews' greatest king, David, was himself the result of a mixed marriage. Ruth, his great-grandmother, was a Moabitess and not a Hebrew. Before the Exile, in fact, many among other peoples and nations became members of the covenant community through mixed marriages with Hebrews, and, like Ruth, acknowledged Yahweh as God.

The story of Ruth illustrates also the Hebrew practice of Levirate marriage (Deuteronomy 25[5-10]). If a man died childless, it was the duty of his brother, or male next-of-kin, to marry the widow. The first child born was then the dead man's heir.

The reason for the practice in the first instance was the view that a widow was part of her husband's estate, and should therefore be inherited by his male next-of-kin. This both provided for her protection and maintenance, and prevented her from marrying away into another family. It would also possibly provide a child who could be regarded as the dead man's son and representative in the land of the living, and one who could later, if such were considered needful, continue any mortuary ceremonies required to give the dead man rest among the shades.

In the story, Ruth shows a double devotion, to her mother-in-law Naomi, and to her dead husband. She leaves her own people and goes with Naomi to Bethlehem, the home of her husband's family, ready to conform to the local social customs.

Jonah

Like the story of Ruth, the book of Jonah was written in protest against the increasing exclusiveness of post-exilic official Judaism towards Gentiles. Both books date from about the same period.

The author of Ruth was concerned mainly with the exclusive policy which sought to ban mixed marriages between Jews and Gentiles. The author of Jonah was concerned with the wider exclusiveness which Judaism was adopting towards the Gentile world as a whole. He thought that it was wrong, and indeed contrary to the hopes of many prophets, who saw Judaism as the means of making God known to the rest of the world.

Many had this hope because they believed this was the divine purpose for them – the people specially chosen by God. He was revealing himself to them, and they in turn would make him known to others. His Temple in Jerusalem would be the spiritual centre of the world (see Micah 4^{1-3}; Isaiah 2^{1-4}, 56^7; The Servant Songs; $42^{1, 4}$, $49^{1, 6}$, 52^{15}; Zechariah $8^{22, 23}$).

The book of Jonah is regarded by most scholars as an allegory with a missionary message to Jews. It is set in the days when Assyria was the dominant power, and its capital, Nineveh, aptly represents the Gentile world.

Jonah (John) felt the call of God to go to Nineveh as a missionary. Like the Jews of his own day, Jonah tried to turn away from God's call, and even to escape it by sailing away in the opposite direction. But he could not escape. Inside a great fish he had time to think, and to ask God for a second chance.

This was a picture of what was happening to the chosen people. They had often refused to listen to God's call, they had been unfaithful to him, they had been swallowed up for fifty years in exile in the great Babylon. Now, says the writer to the exclusive Jews of his day, you are being given a second chance by God to fulfil the purpose for which he chose you, and to proclaim him to the world.

The allegory continues with Jonah, the representative Jew, using his second opportunity, and conducting his mission in Nineveh. To his surprise the people listen and repent. But now there is another lesson for Jonah to learn – that of God's mercy towards all people. Jonah waits outside the city for the judgment of God to fall upon it. When it does not, Jonah is angry and feels that his visit has been useless. Anticipation of this, he reflects, led him to ignore God's call in the first place.

Jonah's attitude reflected well that of many Jews towards other peoples. Those others would be the people upon whom God's judgment would fall; the Jews, as the Chosen People, would be exempt. The prophets warned against this self-satisfaction.

Amos had gained his hearers' attention by speaking first of judgment upon other nations, and then shattered his hearers' complacency by pronouncing God's judgment upon the Jews themselves for their particular sins (Amos 1 and 2). Isaiah had taught that God would use other nations to chastize Israel (Isaiah 10^5).

The last of the prophets, John the Baptist, spoke out against the same attitude towards Gentiles in his day. Judgment was coming upon all, even upon the children of Abraham (Luke 3$^{7,\ 8}$). In the synagogue at Nazareth, when Jesus dared to remind the congregation that God had shown mercy to people who were not Jews, such as the widow of Zarephath and Naaman the Syrian (Luke 4$^{24-30}$), he caused such anger that he was nearly killed.

A plant growing beside Jonah was the means whereby he learned more of the mercy of God. The plant grew quickly, and provided welcome shelter for him from the sun, but not for long. Jonah was angry that such a promising plant could be destroyed by a worm attacking its roots. Then he realized that this was what he wanted God to do to Nineveh. If he could feel concern for a mere plant, which he had not even cultivated, how much greater must be God's mercy towards the thousands of his creation in Nineveh.

Esther

This book presents scholars with many problems. Like other stories with a purpose, the historicity of Esther is slight, but, unlike the others, its religious value is slight also. Its greatest value is probably literary, but that is hardly enough to justify its presence as an official or canonical book of Scripture. Indeed many eminent scholars have not been very happy about the inclusion of this book in the Bible, for even the name of God is omitted, though some Jews have tried to insert it. What then is its purpose? Quite simply, it is intended to give a reason for the existence of a popular Jewish feast – that of Purim or Lots. One problem is, which came first, the feast or the story? Did the story institute the feast, or was the story merely explaining an existing feast?

The Passover feast had been an ancient observance of thanksgiving for new-born lambs long before the Exodus from Egypt gave it a new and more important meaning for Hebrews. Similarly Christians retained the winter festival of Saturnalia, but gave it new meaning as Christmas. Maybe the book of Esther was written likewise, to turn a heathen festival into a respectable Jewish one. Its observance as such comes very late in Hebrew history, about 135 B.C. Therefore it was not one enjoined by the Law of Moses.

There is much further speculation as to which heathen observance was the probable origin of the Jewish feast. One of the simpler suggestions is that the Babylonian god Marduk and goddess Ishtar have become the Jew Mordecai and Jewess Esther, the prominent characters in the Jewish story. (Both Ishtar and Esther mean 'star'.)

The origin of the name Purim has long been forgotten. The story connects it with an Assyrian word *puru* meaning dice – hence the alternative name of Lots for the feast. Sir James Frazer believed the name Purim to be derived from a Babylonian word *puhru* used in connection with an assembly of the gods, called Zakmuk. This Babylonian festival was held at much the same time of year as that of the Jewish Purim.

The story of Esther is set in the period of the Exile in Babylon, under Persian rule. Therefore Babylonian and Persian folklore and nature festivals do, no doubt, in some way account for this Jewish feast said to date from those days.

Thus the book of Esther is best taken as fiction, a patriotic Jewish novel set against the background of life after the Exile for Jews who did not return to Palestine. Unlike the story of Jonah with its wider appeal, that of Esther emphasizes the growing exclusiveness of Judaism. Jonah realized something of the divine compassion for the sinners in Nineveh, but there is no such compassion shown to the enemies of the Jews in the story of Esther. There is satisfaction that those who had plotted against the Jews were themselves slain. The cry at the feast, 'Blessed be Mordecai, Cursed be Haman', was no less than a slogan equivalent to 'Up with the Jews, and down with our enemies'.

The festival is kept as an occasion of thanksgiving for deliverance from enemies, not merely those of the time of the Exile, but those encountered throughout Jewish history, its deepest meaning being the triumph of Judaism.

In some way the story symbolizes all opposition to Judaism, represented by Haman, all persecuted and suffering Jews in the person of Mordecai, and the attractiveness and dignity of the Jewish faith in a Gentile world seen in the beautiful Jewess Esther, who outshone all rivals for the king's attention.

It is interesting to note that, in a male dominated society, the patriotism is shown by a woman, who risks her life in order to save her people.

The story must be taken as a novel, and not as history, since it does not stand up to analysis: it is full of discrepancies. King Ahasuerus, or Xerxes, did not have a wife named Esther; Mordecai could not have lived from the time of the first deportation into Babylon in 597 B.C. until his promotion in 474 B.C.; and Esther could hardly have hoped to conceal her Jewish nationality.

But such probings merely spoil the story, as they would many other works of literature. What we have is a pagan festival found by the Jewish community in Persia, given a new meaning, by a clever conversion of Babylonian myth, and the name Purim or Lots. The story tries to account for the name of the feast (Esther 3⁷). The plotters cast lots to find a suitable day for slaying the Jews – a bit far-fetched, but does fiction always need to be logical?

Job

The author of this book is unknown, but he probably wrote in about 400 B.C. Job, the chief character in the book, is set in the age of the Patriarchs, and is living in the land of Uz, very likely part of northern Arabia.

It is possible that Job was not entirely a character of fiction, but a legendary figure of ancient folklore, rather like the English Robin Hood or King Arthur. A certain amount of legend often springs from actual fact. This material the author, or rather poet, used as the basis of his book. It appears in the prose sections that begin and end it (Job 1–2, 42⁷⁻¹⁷).

As a piece of literature the composition is unique. In a way it is drama, but not action drama. The characters are more like members of a panel, taking part in a public discussion perhaps, and each expressing a point of view in answer to a question about the reason for innocent suffering. Like such a panel, the book of Job explores the question, but does not exhaust it. Nor does it reach any real conclusion.

As late as New Testament times, sickness and suffering were regarded as the direct result of sin. By healing a paralysed man, Jesus demonstrated that the man's sins were forgiven (Mark 2¹⁻¹²). When Jesus was about to heal a man blind from birth, the disciples assumed that his affliction was caused by either his own sin, or that of his parents. Jesus said that it was neither (John 9¹⁻³).

Disasters were regarded in the same way. Some Galileans slain by Pilate, some workmen killed on a construction site, were regarded as sinners. Jesus pointed out that they were no more guilty than the rest of the nation (Luke 13¹⁻⁵).

The belief that sickness and suffering were the direct result of sin forms the background argument of the book of Job. People believed that God's reward for faithfulness came in the form of material benefits in this life. A long and prosperous life was thus a sign of righteousness. There was so much uncertainty about survival after death, no less of an active future life, that this world seemed to be the only place for God's rewards.

This outlook forms the basis of the opinions expressed by Job's 'comforters'. Job, bereft of his health and possessions, even of his children, has but to repent and God will restore all. (A principle of Christian theology is foreshadowed here – that forgiveness brings restoration, though not as Job's friends understood it. Cf. the Prodigal Son.)

The writer of the book of Job was not satisfied with the conventional outlook. He, like others, was asking: Why do the wicked prosper? Why do the innocent suffer? Ultimately these questions were to lead to a belief in life after death, for divine justice was not always seen to be done in this world. But, despite his search for a deeper understanding, the writer was still unable to find any reward for Job's constancy other than material prosperity in this life.

A number of interesting lines of thought are opened up by the book. It is easy to be faithful to God when all goes well, but adversity is the real test of faith. Many a sufferer has cried out like Job: What have I done to deserve this? Many such, in their anguish, have reproached God for his apparent lack of justice and mercy. Job's message to them is one of trust in the ultimate goodness of God, even though for a time it is not evident. Job himself remained constant under his sufferings because he knew that God would vindicate someone who had always been faithful to him.

Thus the story of Job is timeless. He represents everyone who cries out: Why did it happen to me? Like Jonah and Esther, he may represent his own suffering people, faithful Israel, crying to God: Why did this happen to us? He also represents the firm belief of the prophets that after suffering would come restoration.

One unknown writer carried the subject of innocent suffering further still. This writer lived during the Exile, and his poems are preserved in the book of Isaiah (see p. 24). He described a Servant of God who would suffer innocently for the sins of his people. The writer, for his part, saw that innocent sufferings might indeed be God's way of salvation. People would think, as did Job's comforters, that the Servant was suffering for his own sins, but in reality he was 'stricken for the transgression of my people' (Isaiah 52$^{13-15}$, 53).

It is noteworthy that the idea of God's achieving his purpose through suffering, rather than through judgment and a display of physical power, was born during the suffering nation's captivity in Babylon.

Both the book of Job and the Suffering Servant poems point forward to the New Testament. The Christian revelation does not entirely solve the problem. Nevertheless it does give reassurance that innocent suffering is part of the redemptive purpose of God, as the writer of the Servant poems thought that it might be.

The role of Messiah favoured by Jesus was much influenced by the Servant poems. He carried the point of suffering beyond that of Job. Jesus was the truly righteous man, crying out after the manner of Job: 'My God, my God, why hast thou forsaken me?' But, more than Job, even death would not shake his constancy. The Resurrection was essential in order to assure all those whom Job represents that God does vindicate the righteous, and that the wicked do not ultimately prosper.

8. Miracles in the Old Testament

National

The Hebrews believed in God, and in his special interest in their affairs. Consequently they interpreted all their experiences as being indications of either his favour or displeasure. This made them prone to see the hand of God directly at work upon all occasions, and to record them accordingly, although usually long after the incidents occurred, and after much oral transmission. It may well be that God acted through natural laws rather than against them; but, granted his existence, who is to say, with our still limited knowledge, that he always did, or does?

So we approach the subject of Old Testament miracles with some degree of caution, but with minds not closed against the possibility that some remarkable things happened, and that God in some way was responsible for them. God is not removed from the scene merely because it is found that he was perhaps making use of nature, and not acting contrary to it.

The Old Testament is superb drama, and drama is often larger than life, which is not the same thing as its being untrue. It is human drama and divine drama, played upon the stage of Canaan. Some of it is sordid, some of it sublime. The reader of the Old Testament is given a panorama of Hebrew history by a team of researchers, dramatists, editors, compilers, etc. At times the production team lets the spotlight fall to draw special attention to a particular incident or an important individual. This is when the miraculous appears.

The spotlight, as it were, reminds the reader that this is not merely human drama. God is at work in the affairs of men. He is revealing his greatness. This is what makes the Old Testament so much more than a mere historical play. This is the essential message of the Old Testament and its writers.

It is very important that a student of the Old Testament should realize that it is the overall divine interest and concern that matters in the drama, not any ability on our part to check, or to explain with precision, any particular miracle, or indeed any incidental part of it. The writers were proud, not merely of their nation, but of their God. They believed that, alongside the human drama of their own history, the drama of divine revelation was also unfolding, from tribal god to Universal Creator.

The book of Genesis forms the prologue of Hebrew history. Act one of the nation's drama begins with the book of Exodus. The central character there is Moses, portrayed as God's agent in the great escape. As a baby his life is preserved, and he is given the name Moses by Pharaoh's daughter, who adopted him. This is by way of introduction. The association in the margin of R.S.V Exodus 2^{10} of the Hebrew Mosheh, Moses, with the Hebrew *mashah*, meaning to draw out, supports the traditional meaning of the name as saved from water, but it seems unlikely that an Egyptian princess would think along these Hebrew lines. An alternative suggestion is that the name is of Egyptian origin and simply means born which, in a sense, well describes Moses unusual arrival in the story.

It is while Moses is on Mount Sinai (or Horeb), minding sheep for his father-in-law, that the spotlight first falls. It is directed upon a 'burning bush', and Moses becomes conscious of God's calling him to rescue his people in Egypt. It does not matter in the least whether a bush could be aflame without burning away, whether it was something to do with Sinai's being a volcano, or whether it was a shaft of sunlight lighting upon an autumn tree. For Moses it was a spiritual experience, and such are not meant for analysis. It is Moses' conviction that he is being called by God that is important (see *Sacred trees* p. 82).

Moses returns to Egypt, and, together with Aaron his brother, begins negotiations with the Pharaoh. The spotlight falls again, for this is not merely negotiation on the human level. Yahweh is proving himself to be stronger than the gods of Egypt.

It was very fortunate for the Hebrews that a series of natural disasters (none of the sources of the Pentateuch contains more than eight) lent weight to the negotiations. The Hebrews, living in a separate community, escaped the worst of them. Finally, plague broke out, 'and there was a great cry in Egypt, for there was not a house where one was not dead' (Exodus 12^{30}). But how much more dramatic to say that it was the firstborn. The firstborn had special significance for the Hebrews.

The 'miracle' of the escape was the crossing of the Red Sea, not the sea of that name in a modern atlas, but the Yam Suph (Heb.) now known as the Gulf of Akaba. This was the great moment in Hebrew history, and one would expect it to be highlighted. It was, they felt, a triumph for their God. So the Elizabethans interpreted the gales that harassed the Spanish Armada. Their commemorative medal bore the words, in Latin, 'the Lord blew and they were scattered', in allusion to Exodus 10.

The crossing was not perhaps the miracle that the Hebrews believed it to be. Volcanic earth tremors, tide or 'strong east wind' (Exodus 14^{21})

are suggested as explanations. Indeed, in December 1931, a gale blew the tide out of the Thames estuary at Southend to such a degree that there was not enough water to float the barges. If such could happen in the Thames, it could certainly happen in the Gulf of Akaba. But how fortunate for the Hebrews that, whatever it was, it happened when it did, and not a week sooner or a week later. That perhaps was the miracle.

The capture of the strategic city of Jericho, commanding all central Canaan, was the first great victory for the invading Hebrews. Again the spotlight on the drama! Although there were fords for crossing the Jordan river (Joshua 2⁷), a special crossing, like that of the Red Sea, brought the Hebrews to the plains of Jericho. Before the attack Joshua met the 'commander of the army of the Lord' who assured him of victory (Joshua 5¹³–6⁷).

Then began a war of nerves, lasting for a week and involving the mystic number seven. The defenders of Jericho were not ready for the attack when finally it came. Some of the walls crumbled, there were already traitors inside, and the resistance of the inhabitants was low (Joshua 6). Since the house of Rahab remained intact the falling flat of the wall would seem to be literary hyperbole designed to indicate the ease and completeness of the victory.

To the great Elijah the worship of Yahweh seemed in danger of extinction. A new foreign cult of Melkart worship had been introduced into Israel by Queen Jezebel. It was fast gaining hold. Elijah arranged a trial of strength between Melkart and Yahweh. It was to take place on Mount Carmel. Two sacrifices were prepared, and the god who was the stronger was to answer by igniting one. The Melkart priests called upon their god first. All day long nothing happened. In the evening Elijah prayed to Yahweh. 'Then the fire of the Lord fell, and consumed the burnt offering . . .' (1 Kings 18³⁸). The people were convinced and said, 'The Lord, he is God' (1 Kings 18³⁹). Appropriately, Elijah's own name meant 'Yahweh is God'.

What exactly happened on Mount Carmel it is impossible to tell, nor does it matter. Somehow Elijah convinced the Hebrews that Yahweh was their God, and not Melkart. The 'fire of the Lord' usually meant lightning. There had been a long drought, and this was always a sign of divine displeasure. Shortly after the sacrifice on Mount Carmel there was a storm. Thus Yahweh ended the drought. This in itself was perhaps what convinced them. Indeed there is a connection between the sacrifice described and ancient sympathetic magic, in this case rain-making. Elijah poured out water as though this was a hint to the heavens (1 Kings 18³³⁻³⁵).

Personal

It is not surprising that notable individuals like Elijah should have gathered marvels around them. Hebrew tradition itself may well have confused both Elijah and Elisha, for similar stories have gathered round each. It would be wrong, however, to suggest that none was genuine. Saintly people have often possessed unusual powers and knowledge.

Maybe Elisha's raising of the Shunammite woman's son was the result of the 'kiss of life' (2 Kings 4$^{34, 35}$), maybe it was a miracle. Certainly the story in 2 Kings 1 of Elijah's sitting on the top of a hill, calling down fire upon each squad of fifty sent to arrest him, and the fate of the forty-two small boys in 2 Kings 2, seem to be over-dramatic ways of gaining respect; but the real importance of Elijah and Elisha lies not in whether the marvel stories around them are true or accurate, but in the stand that the prophets made against the threat to Yahweh religion from a foreign deity. Their work was to overthrow the family of King Ahab, who encouraged it, and to put a new dynasty upon the throne. Thus their endeavours to achieve this, and their encouragement to Jehu to seize the throne, have come to be referred to as the prophetic revolution (1 Kings 19$^{15-18}$; 2 Kings 9, 10$^{18-31}$).

Moses and Aaron also have their share of personal wonders. Rods were very useful for giving signs to the Pharaoh, for parting waters, and for obtaining water from rocks – conjurers and water-diviners still use them (Exodus 8^7, 14^{16}, 17$^{5-9}$).

Joshua's victory over the Amorite king (Joshua 10) was commemorated in a National Song (preserved in a collection known as the Book of Jashar), a verse of which is incorporated by the editors into the prose account (Joshua 10$^{12, 13}$). Joshua wished that the day might last long enough for him to gain victory. In poetry this becomes a dramatic command to the sun to stand still. Everyone knows how some days remain light longer than others. An alternative is that Joshua wished the night to last, and the sun not to rise, until victory was won.

Samson, the semi-legendary Hebrew Hercules, is said to have done some extraordinary things. His stories are very much of folk origin. Through him the Hebrew people were getting at their new enemy, the Philistines. He symbolized the spirit of Hebrew resistance. His pranks upon the Philistines kept up, as it were, the Hebrew morale.

Was Samson's strength in his hair, or was it really in his principles, which his hair symbolized? His hair was uncut because of his Nazerite vow. When he kept his vow he was strong, at least with a moral strength. When his vow was broken through his own weakness, his physical strength went also. God is shown as standing by him, therefore, only when he is true to his principles.

Topographical

Some biblical marvels are possibly attempts to explain the presence of some object or physical feature. The British Isles alone are full of oddities of nature, or antiquity, and plenty of fantastic legends have grown up around them. And it is important to remember that although the Hebrew historians, from our point of view, lived a long time ago they too had an ancient history to look back upon. They too had a semi-historical, semi-legendary past. A frequent comment by their historians, after offering some explanation about an object or place, was that it was 'there to this day' (Joshua 4[9]; 2 Samuel 6[8]).

There are two notable Old Testament explanations of the origin of some prehistoric stones. Just over the river Jordan, not far from Jericho, was Gilgal (*gal* is a name meaning stone circle). The story of Joshua's ordering that stones be placed on the bank of the Jordan to mark the place where the Hebrews crossed (Joshua 4) may well be an attempt to explain the existence of a stone circle or stone cairn which had already been there for centuries.

Near the Dead Sea a standing stone (menhir), either placed there by prehistoric man, or caused by rock erosion and caked with salt from the winds of the Dead Sea, possibly gave rise to the legend that Lot's wife was turned to a pillar of salt because she looked back (Genesis 19[26]). (One is reminded of the fateful looking back of Orpheus.)

Lot's wife looked back on the destruction of Sodom and Gomorrah, the cities of the valley. The charred ruins of two deserted cities demanded an explanation from the Hebrew historians. Legend had it that once, in the time of Abraham, the cities had been great and prosperous, yet tragedy had befallen them. There was always one simple explanation for disaster, as the Hebrews saw it. It was God's punishment for wickedness. Therefore God must have sent the fire (or volcanic eruption) that destroyed those cities, just as he sent the flood to destroy all human beings save Noah and his family. The names Sodom and Gomorrah, synonymous with the idea of wickedness and corruption, have lasted through New Testament times (Matthew 11[23, 24]) until today.

During a religious reform carried out by Hezekiah, King of Judah, he destroyed, among other things, a bronze serpent in the Temple. It had become an object of worship, for tradition said that it had been made by Moses (2 Kings 18[4]). The tradition concerning the origin of the bronze serpent may well have grown up in order to explain its presence in the Temple.

The story of its origin is to be found in Numbers 21[4–9]. Among the many hazards of the journey in the wilderness was a plague of 'fiery serpents', that is snakes whose bites caused inflammation. Some people died from the bites. A plague like this, it was thought, must be a punishment from God. However, Moses was said to have made a bronze serpent, and to have put it upon a pole. Those who looked at it would live. Incidentally a serpent has been a symbol of healing from very ancient times. A serpent entwining the staff of Aesculapius, the mythological god of medicine, forms the badge of the Royal Army Medical Corps.

This particular legend seems to be another example of sympathetic magic. A serpent is made in order to cure the sting of a serpent, in the same way as Elijah poured out water in order to obtain rain.

Another interesting example of this occurs in the story of the return by the Philistines to the Hebrews of the Ark of the Covenant. Misfortune befell the Philistines while the Ark was in their hands after its capture. A plague of mice led to a plague among humans, which involved tumours and resulted in death. Five golden tumours and five golden mice were made, one of each to represent the five principal Philistine cities. The golden models were put into the Ark, and it was sent away, also carrying with it, it was hoped, the plague (1 Samuel 5 and 6). In fact it spread to the men of Beth-shemesh, who received the Ark upon its return.

This chapter does not attempt to deal with every marvel reported in the Old Testament, but merely to show how one needs to approach the different types. However legendary they may be, they serve as a reminder of the Hebrews' conviction that God was actively at work in their history.

9. Primitive Religious Beliefs

Even in the twentieth century primitive religious beliefs linger on in the form of superstitions. Though the religion of their origin may be obsolete, yet they still have a surprising hold upon some people. It was the practice of the Christian Church in its early days to christianize rather than abolish existing festivals and religious observances. Thus Christmas displaced Saturnalia, some pagan rites of spring still linger on in the Christian ceremonies of Easter, and the Virgin Mary has superseded the mother goddess of the fertility cults.

In much the same way, in the Old Testament, Hebrew religion also passed through its primitive stages of development. Animism lingered on throughout the first half of Old Testament history, followed by the fertility cult of Baal and Ashtoreth. From the invasion of Canaan until the Exile this latter was the great threat to Yahweh worship. Eventually the Hebrews managed to outgrow this stage of religious development, and did so about 500 years ahead of the rest of the world; for in the first century A.D., when Christianity was spreading throughout the Roman Empire, Greek mystery religions, including fertility cults, were in full swing.

Animism

Animism is mankind's earliest stage of religion. It is closely allied to magic. In the very early years of mankind's history the world of nature was full of mystery. Its laws were undiscovered (many still are), and anything not understood was attributed to the supernatural. Belief in the supernatural was instinctive. Man needed some source of strength and courage, other than himself, to help him venture forth into the unknown and often frightening world.

Objects which seemed to possess a life of their own were thought to have spirits dwelling within them. In Greek mythology one is familiar with the idea of dryads, the spirits in trees causing them to move and rustle in the wind. Also familiar is the idea of water spirits, nymphs, and nereids, animating springs, streams, fountains and the sea. The common noun 'volcano' is itself derived from the proper noun 'Vulcan'.

Mountains, although not necessarily showing obvious life, were nevertheless great and majestic, awe-inspiring, dominating, forbidding, dangerous, and therefore possessing power over men. Such places were surely the homes of gods, e.g. Mount Olympus in Greek mythology and Asgard in Norse legend. Mountain tops were far removed from the world of men. They were sometimes white with snow, and covered by clouds, penetrating heaven itself. One can easily understand why a volcano could be regarded as the home of a fire-spirit or god.

Not only mountains but also stones were believed to have indwelling spirits. Stones were arranged in circles, as at Stonehenge or Avebury. Sometimes they were erected singly; or sometimes two upright stones supported a third horizontal one. Prehistoric Palestine also has its share of stone circles, cairns, menhirs and dolmens.

Earlier religious ideas always tend to linger on, and so it is not surprising to find Hebrew religion touched by animism. Although Abraham came from Babylon, a land of moon worship, the early stories of the Old Testament show him, and his descendants, partly animistic in religion.

Sacred trees

In the Old Testament sacred trees are usually oaks or terebinths. Sometimes there was one tree, and sometimes several together in a grove. Sacred trees were used as oracles. A priest, prophet, or prophetess would be in attendance to interpret the message of the tree-spirit for the inquirer. People would sometimes hang gifts upon a sacred tree, as a sort of votive offering.

When Abraham settled in Canaan oracle trees were quite common. These trees were sacred, and it was natural that near them he should feel that God was communicating with him. It was at the oak of Moreh that God promised Abraham: 'To your descendants I will give this land' (Genesis 12$^{6-8}$). The same assurance, and also the promise of a son, was given him as he dwelt by the oaks of Mamre (Genesis 13$^{17, 18}$, 18$^{1-10}$).

After God had renewed his covenant with him, Jacob collected from his family all the images of household gods, teraphim and lucky charms, and buried them under a sacred oak at Shechem. This meant that they could not harm him, because they were now under the power of the tree-spirit (Genesis 35$^{2-4}$). When Deborah, who had been nurse to Rebekah, Jacob's mother, died, she was buried under a sacred tree near Bethel (Genesis 35^8). It was an oak with a special name, *Allon-bacuth*, or the 'oak of weeping'. It was thus named, not because of Deborah, but because it was a place where the rite of weeping for Tammuz took place.

In many parts of the world fertility worship has interpreted the winter season as a time when the mother goddess is mourning for her child (or lover). It is therefore a time when Nature mourns in sympathy. In Babylon, the mother goddess was Ishtar (Astarte or Ashtoreth) and her lover was Tammuz, the sun or vegetation god. Weeping for Tammuz, and the corresponding Rites of Adonis, became acts of worship. (Cf. Ceres and Proserpina or Demeter and Persephone, Aphrodite and Adonis, Cybele and Attis, Isis and Osiris.)

Deborah the prophetess, one of the Judges, 'used to sit under the palm of Deborah' (Judges 4[4, 5]) 'between Ramah and Bethel'. The Israelites came to her for judgment. This means that they came to consult the tree oracle, and Deborah gave the answers.

King Saul, himself possessing prophetic power, sat under a pomegranate tree in Gibeah, and also a tamarisk tree in Ramah (1 Samuel 14[2], 22[6]). The men of Jabesh-gilead, having retrieved his body from the Philistines, buried it under a tamarisk tree (1 Samuel 31[13]).

David 'inquired of the Lord' about an attack upon the Philistines. He was told to listen for the 'sound of marching in the tops of the balsam trees', and then attack. The noise would be the wind in the branches, but to David it was a message from God (2 Samuel 5[23, 24]).

After the division of the kingdom into Israel and Judah, and Jeroboam's having set up shrines at Dan and Bethel in the north, the story is told in 1 Kings 13 of a 'man of God' from Judah, who came to denounce Jeroboam. The 'man of God' was found sitting under an oak, again an oracle tree.

Thus Abraham was not the only one to receive communication from God near a sacred tree. Gideon received a theophany (i.e. a manifestation of God) underneath an oak in Ophrah, and his son Abimelech was made king by the men of Shechem near a sacred oak and pillar (Judges 6[11], 9[6]).

The most notable example in the Old Testament of God's using a tree as a means of communication is that of Moses and the burning bush (Exodus 3). Such a tree was the home of a fire-spirit. Moses was on Mount Horeb, i.e. Sinai (J and E), when he saw it. This in itself was a sacred mountain, a volcano perhaps, somewhere in the land of Midian, where he was in exile.

Further examples may be found in Genesis 21[33]; Judges 9[7-15, 37]; 1 Samuel 10[3].

Sacred waters

Oracle wells, springs, and sacred waters are as widespread in early belief as are sacred trees. In the Bible one meets the expression 'living water', which meant water from a stream or spring, as opposed to water stored in a cistern. Water has so much power, is so essential to life, that it is easy to see why people once regarded it as inhabited by spirits.

In Greek and Roman mythology one is familiar with Poseidon or Neptune, the god of the sea. Of all waters, the sea was surely the most powerful and terrible, with its changing moods from calm to tempest. Streams and rivers also seemed to possess life as they rippled gently or rushed in torrents. Springs and wells, mysteriously renewed, proclaimed an indwelling spirit.

Remains of this belief are to be found in the ordeal by water of mediaeval times. A prisoner, particularly if accused of witchcraft, was thrown into water and judged guilty if he floated. This was regarded as a sign that the water of his baptism had rejected him. Belief in the healing power of water is well known even up to the present day, although this is now more usually ascribed to its chemical rather than its spiritual content, yet spiritual efficacy is believed to be inherent in holy water, and in some at least of the numerous forms of baptism found throughout the world.

Wells and springs were, of course, of supreme importance to nomadic people. Consequently we find frequent mention of oracle wells in the Old Testament. One of the oldest fragments of Hebrew poetry has been preserved in the book of Numbers. It is known as the 'Song of the Well', and the well is addressed as though it were a person rather than a thing. 'Spring up, O well! – Sing to it!' (Numbers 21[17].)

In Genesis 14[7] there is mention of En-mishpat, which means the 'spring of decision or judgment'. It was to be found in Kadesh, which itself means 'consecrated'; i.e. it was a sanctuary or holy place, where people could consult a divine oracle.

Another sacred well is associated with Hagar, the maidservant of Abraham, and the mother of his son Ishmael. When she fled from the jealous Sarah, 'the angel of the Lord found her by a spring of water in the wilderness' .The oracle told her to return to her mistress. The well was named Beer-lahai-roi, the well of the god who sees, or who makes himself seen (Genesis 16[14]). An *el* had revealed himself at a particular location, and so it became sacred (see p. 19).

When Hagar was again banished she wandered in the wilderness of Beersheba, the most southerly point of Palestine. Beersheba means either 'seven wells', or the 'well of seven spirits', or the 'well of the oath' (Genesis 21[14]). Here Abraham planted a tamarisk tree, and 'called there on the name of the Lord' (Genesis 21[33], 26[32, 33]).

When the Hebrew tribes settled in Canaan one of the boundaries of Judah lay 'along to the waters of En-shemesh' (Joshua 15[7]), which means the 'spring of the sun'. This was probably an oracle of the sun god. The tribe of Simeon settled further south, as far as Baalath-beer, the 'mistress of the spring' (Joshua 19[8]).

Gideon and his men camped beside Harod, the 'spring of trembling'. Here God spoke to him, and told him to say to his men: 'Whoever is fearful and trembling, let him return home' (Judges 7[1-3]).

A number of wells dated back to the days of totemism, and were dedicated to sacred animals, e.g. En-gedi, the spring of the kid (2 Chronicles 20[2]); Eglaim, the spring of the two calves (Isaiah 15[8]); and the Jackal's Well mentioned by Nehemiah (Nehemiah 2[13]).

A curious story is told in Genesis 32[22-32] of Jacob's wrestling with a 'man' during the night, as he was crossing the Jabbok river. The river-spirit was thus trying to prevent Jacob from crossing over. The incident ended at daybreak, because then the spirit would have to vanish. There were perhaps several reasons why this story was told. It gives a reason for the change of Jacob's name to Israel, i.e. 'one who strives with God' (source J). Also it suggests an origin for the Jewish food law concerning the hip sinew. Finally it provides a possible explanation for a place named Peniel – 'face of God' (cf. Genesis 35[9-13]: source P account).

Sacred mountains and rocks

The most notable sacred mountain in the Old Testament is, of course, Mount Sinai (sources J and P), or Horeb (sources E and D). At this mountain Moses received his call from God to help his people in Egypt. Here God presented himself as 'I am what I am', i.e. Yahweh, the God of Abraham, Isaac, and Jacob (Exodus 3[14]).

To this same mountain Moses brought the Hebrew slaves after the Exodus from Egypt. With great solemnity he gathered the people together at the foot of the mountain, with strict orders not to touch it because it was holy. There he introduced them to the God who had rescued them from slavery. He would be their God, if they would be his people.

A solemn agreement or covenant was made, the Decalogue and the Book of the Covenant providing the basic terms. Two stones from the sacred mountain (whether engraved or not) were carried in the Ark in order that God's presence could go with his people (cf. 2 Kings 5[17]).

The prophet Elijah fled to Mount Horeb after the slaughter of the prophets of Baal (1 Kings 19[8-18]), and, after violent storms and earthquakes, God spoke to him there in a still small voice.

The location of the original Sinai of the Old Testament is a matter of some speculation. It is most unlikely to have been the present mountain of that name, on the peninsula between the Gulf of Akaba and the Gulf of Suez. The holy mountain described in Exodus 19 and 1 Kings 19[11-12] was possibly a volcano. This may indeed have some bearing upon the 'burning bush' theophany, and upon the pillar of cloud by day and of fire by night (Exodus 3[1-6], 13[21], 14[19]).

The present Mount Sinai was never a volcano, but, in the land of Midian and Edom, at the northern end of the Gulf of Akaba, there were volcanoes. This was the part of the country in which Moses was a shepherd, which he knew well, and where he received his call from God. It was also the district, on the verge of the Promised Land, where the Hebrew tribes spent so much of the wilderness period.

At his call (Exodus 3[12]) Moses was told by God: 'When you have brought forth the people out of Egypt, you shall serve God upon this mountain'. A route due east from Goshen to Midian was a much more likely one for the escaping slaves than a long route around a peninsula. Evidence also points to the Gulf of Akaba as being the water crossed by them. Only in English translations is it called the Red Sea (1 Kings 9[26]). The original was to be found in the land of Edom, and was known in Hebrew as Yam Suph, meaning 'sea of reeds'.

There are many other mountains with sacred associations mentioned in the Old Testament, for every community had its 'high place' devoted to Baal worship.

Another notable mountain connected with Yahweh worship was Mount Carmel. It was there that Elijah challenged the prophets of Melkart, the Phoenician Baal, to a duel by sacrifice, and, in some sort of theophany, Yahweh declared himself the rightful God of Israel (1 Kings 18[30-40]). Even before this, it was a place for Yahweh worship (1 Kings 18[30]).

Mounts Nebo and Pisgah were mountains where tradition maintained that Moses viewed the land of Canaan, and where he died (Deuteronomy 32[49, 50], 34[1]). Also on Mount Pisgah, Balaam offered sacrifice for Balak, King of Moab, in the hope of cursing the advancing Hebrews. An attempt also took place on Mount Peor (belonging to the Baal of Peor) and the high place of Bamoth-baal (Numbers 22[41], 23[14, 15], 23[28]-24[1]). Other sacred mountains include Tabor, Gibeah, and Gelah.

Next to mountains came the belief that some stones were inhabited by spirits. This was the reason why hewing stone to make an altar was forbidden (Exodus 20[25]). Boundary stones, whether natural or devised, were especially regarded in this light.

The best known example in the Old Testament of this belief is that of Jacob resting upon his pillow of stone, and receiving a vision of angels, in the course of which God's promises to Abraham and Isaac were renewed for himself. In the morning Jacob realized that he had slept on a holy mountain, and upon an inhabited stone. He therefore poured out an offering by way of apology to the indwelling spirit for the inadvertent sacrilege. Tradition maintained that this was the origin of the sanctuary at Beth-el, meaning the 'house of God'. The spirit was then known as the El-Beth-el, i.e. the God of Bethel (Genesis 28$^{11-22}$). Jacob also set up a stone pillar on the grave of Rachel, his favourite wife (Genesis 35^{20}).

When Jacob was reconciled with his uncle Laban, they made a cairn of stones (source J), and erected a single pillar of stone (source E), to mark the place where they made a covenant not to trespass upon each other's property or possessions. The spirit within the stone would watch, to see that Jacob and Laban never again cheated each other. 'The Lord watch between you and me, when we are absent one from the other.' The pillar was called Mizpah, i.e. 'Watchpost', and the heap, Galeed, meaning the 'Heap of Witness' (Genesis 31$^{44-54}$).

Another stone heap or cairn was, according to tradition, made by Joshua, to mark the point where the Hebrews crossed the Jordan (Joshua 4$^{19-24}$). There was evidently a stone heap or circle at Gilgal, and this was said to be its origin. It was quite important because Saul's coronation took place there (1 Samuel 10^8, 11$^{14-15}$). Also he offered sacrifice there before battles with the Philistines and the Amalekites (1 Samuel 13^8, 15^{12}).

Joshua also erected a pillar under a sacred oak in the sanctuary at Shechem, to mark the solemn renewal of the Covenant between Yahweh and his people (Joshua 24$^{26, 27}$). The spirit within the stone was to act as witness: 'Behold, this stone shall be a witness against us; for it has heard all the words of the Lord which he spoke to us . . .'

When the Hebrews were gathering forces against the Philistines in the days of Samuel, they camped at a stone called Ebenezer, the 'stone of help' (1 Samuel 4^1, 5^1). Samuel himself was said to be responsible for raising the stone (1 Samuel 7^{12}) and naming it, saying, 'hitherto the Lord has helped us'.

After the capture of the Ark by the Philistines, disasters befell them, and plans were made for its return. A new cart was prepared, and oxen to draw it. When it arrived back in Hebrew territory it stopped spontaneously at a great stone. The Hebrews at Beth-shemesh took this to be a special sign, and the oxen were offered as a burnt offering to the Lord (1 Samuel 6^{14}).

Abimelech slew his seventy half-brothers 'upon one stone', and was then made king 'by the oak of the pillar at Shechem' (Judges 9$^{5-6}$).

Sacred stones, of which these are but a few examples, were very common in ancient times. Standing in front of Solomon's Temple were two pillars of bronze. They did not support any part of the building, but may have been a survival of the ancient stone pillars (1 Kings 7$^{15-22}$).

The Assyrians, Babylonians and Phoenicians also had pillars at the entrances to their temples.

Human sacrifice

In ancient civilizations human sacrifice was a common practice. When great favours were sought from the gods, or atonement was required, the costliest offerings had to be made. Often the sacrifices were of children, particularly the firstborn.

Such a sacrifice would be made by a king before battle, or even as a regular act of worship to ensure the good will of the gods towards a community. Sometimes a child was sacrificed by being placed beneath the foundations of important buildings – city gates and city walls (Joshua 6[26]).

Since Hebrew history emerges from ancient civilizations and ancient religious beliefs, examples of human sacrifice occur in the Old Testament, but not in connection with Hebrew religion.

Hebrew religion itself never required human sacrifice. From the making of the Covenant onwards it formed no part of Yahweh worship. In this respect Hebrew religion was already moving forward beyond that of contemporary cults.

The story of Abraham's attempt to offer his son Isaac to Yahweh is important because it shows that this sort of worship was not required by him. An animal offering would do as a substitute (Genesis 22). There was, of course, nothing unusual in Abraham's belief that God might desire him to offer his son: it was a practice with which he must have been very familiar.

Yet, despite its disregard of human sacrifice, Hebrew religion did regard human firstborn males as God's property, and needing some redemption (Exodus 13[2]). The firstborn son was originally redeemed by a substitute animal offering, as in the case of Isaac; but in time this was displaced by the payment of five shekels to the Temple and a presentation ceremony (Luke 2[22, 23]).

The firstborn of animals also were due to God, but they too could often be redeemed, e.g. a firstborn ass could be redeemed by a lamb (Exodus 13[12, 13], 34[19, 20]). The feast of Weeks celebrated the first fruits of the wheat harvest (Exodus 34[22]). The Passover originated as a festival of thanksgiving for new-born lambs, involving the sacrifice of some of them. The Exodus from Egypt gave it new significance; but still the sacrifice of a male lamb played a prominent part, even into New Testament times.

The fact that Hebrew religion did not require human sacrifice did not stop the Hebrews from practising it when they indulged in Baal worship.

Child-burning frequently took place, even beneath the walls of Jerusalem, in the Valley of Hinnom, where Molech was worshipped. In 627 B.C., as part of his reformation, King Josiah defiled Molech's shrine and forbade child sacrifice (2 Kings 23¹⁰). His action was prompted by the finding in the Temple of a law book, which was probably Deuteronomy. This condemned human sacrifice (Deuteronomy 18¹⁰).

This particular shrine was condemned by Jeremiah, who insisted that Yahweh wanted no such sacrifice (Jeremiah 7³¹, 19⁵). Ezekiel took the view that Yahweh allowed it in order to horrify his people, so that they might realize that he was their God (Ezekiel 20²⁶).

In surrounding tribes and kingdoms examples of human sacrifice appear not infrequently in the Old Testament. When Israel was fighting against Moab, its king, Mesha, saw that the battle was going against him. 'Then he took his eldest son who was to reign in his stead, and offered him for a burnt offering upon the wall. And there came great wrath upon Israel; and they withdrew from him and returned to their own land' (2 Kings 3²⁷). After such a sacrifice the Hebrews no doubt felt that they had little chance of success.

The Gibeonites, a tribe closely associated with Israel since the time of Joshua (Joshua 9³⁻¹⁵), required from David the death of seven sons of King Saul, because he had violated Joshua's treaty with them. King David granted their request. Three years of famine had apparently indicated God's displeasure, and Saul's violation of the treaty was regarded as the cause. The Gibeonites were members of the Covenant People, and the sacrifice of Saul's sons was offered to Yahweh. 'They hanged them on the mountain before the Lord, and the seven of them perished together' (2 Samuel 21⁹). And since, after the sacrifice, rain fell, it looked as if the divine displeasure *had* been appeased.

The editors of the books of Kings ascribed the fall of the Northern Kingdom of Israel to their people's unfaithfulness to God, and indulgence in foreign worship, including causing their sons and daughters to pass through the fire, very probably as human sacrifices (2 Kings 17¹⁷). The peoples brought into the north by the Assyrians to colonize it, after the deportation of most of the Hebrews, also burnt their children to Adrammelech and Anammelech (2 Kings 17³¹). Among the evils practised by King Manasseh of Judah was that of making his son pass through the fire (2 Kings 21⁶).

Holiness

Holiness has become a word associated with saintly people and sacred things. A holy person is someone striving after moral perfection and pureness of heart. Goodness and holiness go together. Holy things are those set apart for religious purposes.

Thus in the Old Testament Isaiah frequently referred to Yahweh as the Holy One of Israel, and in his vision of God heard the seraphim singing, 'Holy, holy, holy, is the Lord of hosts' (Isaiah 6^3, 10^{20}). In the presence of Yahweh's perfection the prophet was conscious of his own sinfulness, and that of his people. It was this perfection which set Yahweh apart and made him holy.

Most deities worshipped in the ancient world were super-human in character, with human temperaments and human failings. People had to be careful to approach a god when his mood was good, or to put him in a benevolent state of mind by offering sacrifice. The gods were like the people who worshipped them.

But not so did Yahweh come to be known. He was different, and those who worshipped him were expected to resemble him in character. Thus in the Hebrew Law came the command: 'You shall be holy; for I the Lord your God am holy' (Leviticus 19^2).

The idea of holiness as indicating moral perfection was quite a late development. In early Hebrew thought it had no such connection. It was an indefinable something, not unlike the 'uncleanness' of the New Testament, with which people could become infected. It is possibly best described by a modern comparison.

We are all familiar with the idea of radioactivity. Objects and substances can become radioactive. They then give off a power which is called radioactivity. People handling such things have to take strict precautions and wear protective clothing. Anything coming into contact with a radioactive substance would itself become radioactive, and therefore dangerous.

In a similar way holiness was thought of as being given off by a sacred object. A god was surrounded by holiness. It caused people to keep their distance, and was a form of taboo. It was not a desirable quality, and it was highly contagious from object to object and from person to person. If it got out of control, destruction of the object or person affected was the only remedy.

This is why Moses would not allow any person or animal to touch Mount Sinai. It was God's home and therefore holy. Anyone who did not keep the command would be put to death, so that holiness might not spread throughout the camp (Exodus $19^{12, 13}$). Moses himself could ascend the mountain. He was privileged, as were all those who led the nation in worship, and so had to come into contact with holy things.

This was probably the early reason for a priesthood. But even the priest wore protective clothing when engaged in holy work. This is the origin of priestly vestments. The protective clothing was afterwards removed, and, after ritual washing, a form of decontamination, a priest could once again mix with others (Leviticus $16^{4, 23, 28}$).

The Old Testament contains some interesting examples of this primitive conception of holiness. The best known incident, though seldom recognized as such, is that of Moses' call by God through a burning bush. Moses realized that he was in the presence of God, and felt that he was being told therefore to keep his distance, for not only was the bush holy with the divine presence, but so also was the ground surrounding it. Moses was told to take off his shoes (as Moslems still do on entering a mosque), not merely as a sign of reverence but because, if his shoes became infected with holiness, he would trample the infection away with him (Exodus 3⁵; cf. Joshua 5¹⁵).

A tragic example of the fear of holiness comes in the account of the attempt to capture Ai. Joshua and his men had great success with their first major conquest, the city of Jericho. The entire city had been destroyed, save for Rahab and her family because she had helped the invaders. The reason for such wholesale destruction was the belief that this was the way to 'devote' the city to one's god. As it was assigned to the god, all in it became holy, and thus needed to be destroyed (Joshua 6¹⁸, ¹⁹).

The Hebrews shared this early belief, and when they failed to take the much smaller city of Ai a religious reason was sought. Their God had not granted victory. What had offended him? What had gone wrong? Joshua suspected that the ban on devoted things had been broken. Indeed it is possible that information to this effect had already reached him.

Joshua held a public inquiry. The whole community was summoned to appear before him, tribe by tribe. From the guilty tribe of Judah he selected the guilty family and the guilty household. Finally he confronted Achan, the suspect, who broke down and confessed that he had removed plunder from the city (Joshua 7¹⁶⁻²¹).

The penalty was the destruction of Achan, his family, and his possessions, not for disobedience or stealing only, but because he and his household were infected with holiness, and such contamination had to be removed from the camp (Joshua 7²²⁻²⁶).

How factual the story is it is difficult to say. It may have been told to explain the presence of a cairn of stones in the valley of Achor, meaning 'valley of trouble' (Joshua 7²⁶).

The second attempt to take Ai was successful. Thirty thousand men were used. The mere three thousand used at first would seem to be a likely reason for the initial defeat (Joshua 7⁴, 8³).

Another sad example may also have originated by way of explaining a place name – Perezuzzah, meaning the 'breaking forth upon Uzzah' (2 Samuel 6⁸). Since the Ark of the Covenant had been returned by the Philistines, it had stayed in the house of Abinadab (1 Samuel 7¹, ²).

His son Eleazar was consecrated to look after it. Therefore he was permitted to come into contact with holiness.

King David wished to bring the Ark to Jerusalem, his new capital. Plans were made for a civic reception, but something went wrong, which caused David to delay for three months. During this time the Ark was given shelter in another house, that of Obed-edom.

The reason for the postponement was the sudden death of Abinadab's son, Uzzah. The story said that Uzzah, who was not the consecrated son of Abinadab, had touched the Ark, and had died suddenly. Either he had died from shock, or he had been put to death because he had contracted holiness. In any case it was believed that some divine displeasure was indicated, gloom descended upon the proceedings, and the project was postponed (2 Samuel 6$^{1-11}$).

It was possible that Uzzah suddenly died naturally on the day when the Ark was being moved, but superstitious belief was quite enough for Hebrew tradition to forge a direct link between the two events. Perezuzzah would thus get its name, because it was, according to tradition, the place where this had happened (see R.S.V. margin).

Baal worship and high places

Fertility cult is one of the early stages of religious progress the world over. Sex being a dominant factor in all human existence, it is not surprising that it figured prominently in religion. Man's livelihood depended upon fertility among humans, animals and crops. Male and female deities therefore abounded in early religions, and in particular the mother goddess (e.g. Ishtar or Astarte, Ceres or Demeter).

Not the least remarkable thing about Hebrew religious development is that the Hebrew people managed to pass through and beyond the fertility stage of religion about five centuries before any other people. In the early centuries A.D. when Christianity was being preached throughout the Roman Empire, the Greeks and Romans, for all their culture and education, were still at the fertility-cult stage of religion, very elaborate and organized, but, by Jewish standards, none the less primitive.

Many thinking pagans, searching for something nobler, were indeed turning to Judaism, or developing philosophical thought as an alternative. The growing dissatisfaction with fertility cults was a major factor in the early spread of Christianity, although (as already mentioned on page 81) in some quarters traces of fertility cults lingered on in Christian guise.

The Hebrews had gained their spiritual lead only by a long and bitter struggle. It had lasted for the best part of a thousand years, from the time of the settlement in Canaan until the Exile in Babylon.

Upon entering Canaan the Hebrews came into contact with the fertility cult of the land. They too wanted fertility in their new agricultural existence, so they dared not ignore the gods whose special concern this was. It was the task of the prophets to try to draw them away from this.

The male deity was called Baal (plural Baalim, Baals (R.S.V.)) a word meaning Lord or Master. Every district or kingdom had its particular Baal, and some were given special names. The Moabites called their Baal Chemosh; the people of Tyre in Phoenicia named theirs Melkart; Milcom or Molech was the Baal of the Ammonites.

The female deity was Ashtoreth (plural Ashtaroth). The Baals and Ashtaroth were most frequently worshipped on hilltops. These were naturally known as high places, and every town and village had a local one where sacrifices were offered (Judges 2¹³). The Baal was represented by a stone altar, and the Ashtoreth by a grove of trees, a single tree beside the altar, or simply a wooden pole, called an Asherah (plural Asherim).

Gideon, after his call by God, went by night to the local high place, pulled down the altar of Baal, rebuilt it to Yahweh, and offered a bull as a burnt offering, using for wood the Asherah which he had cut down. The people were angry at this act of sacrilege, and demanded Gideon's death. Fortunately his father managed to persuade them that if Baal were a god he would vindicate himself (Judges 6²⁵⁻³²).

It was Hebrew practice also to build stone altars. Abraham had done so on Mount Moriah for his proposed sacrifice of Isaac (Genesis 22⁹). Moses 'built an altar at the foot of the mountain, and twelve pillars, according to the twelve tribes of Israel' (Exodus 24⁴) at the time of the solemn Covenant at Mount Sinai. One of the early Covenant rules was that altars should be made of unhewn stone (Exodus 20²⁵). This rule probably reflects the belief that spirits dwelt in stones, and was a deterrent to the making of graven images.

When Samuel first met Saul he was searching for his father's lost asses. He came to Samuel's city of Ramah when people were preparing for a sacrifice. He was told, as he asked for Samuel: 'Make haste; he has come just now to the city, because the people have a sacrifice today on the high place. As soon as you enter the city, you will find him, before he goes up to the high place to eat' (1 Samuel 9¹², ¹³).

This same story of Saul shows also that some high places had some buildings, in which those who took part in a sacrifice could eat the meat that had been offered (1 Samuel 9²²⁻²⁴). This was the only occasion when people ate meat, until Deuteronomy permitted non-sacrificial slaughter of domestic animals (Deuteronomy 12¹⁵, ¹⁶).

The priests on duty at high places were allowed the first dip with a three-pronged fork into the pot of boiled sacrificial meat. Eli's two sons, Hophni and Phineas, were thought wicked because they did not wish thus to take 'pot luck', and instead selected their joint beforehand for roasting instead of stewing (1 Samuel 2$^{12-17}$).

Ordinary people were easily confused by the sort of worship offered at high places. Sometimes Yahweh was worshipped, and sometimes it was Baal and Ashtoreth, whom they did not wish to ignore because of their especial concern with agriculture. Thus, for ordinary people, Yahweh was in danger of being no more than another Baal, worshipped as Baal would be. The prophets recognized this danger, and continually fought against all corruption of Yahweh worship.

Elijah refused to allow the Baal Melkart to displace Yahweh in Israel. The writing prophets also were sternly against Baal worship, and, growing towards monotheism, poured scorn on these gods, not only because it was useless to turn to them for help, but because they were in fact non-existent.

Jeremiah makes clear the immorality that was associated with Baal worship. 'Yea, upon every high hill and under every green tree you bowed down as a harlot' (Jeremiah 2^{20}).

Jeremiah saw Baal worship, moreover, as a double immorality – that of becoming involved in fertility cult, and Israel's spiritual immorality in deserting Yahweh and going after other gods, like a bride forsaking her husband and seeking other lovers: 'Surely, as a faithless wife leaves her husband, so have you been faithless to me, O house of Israel' (Jeremiah 3^{20}); 'Truly the hills are a delusion, the orgies on the mountains' (Jeremiah 3^{23}). Jeremiah called the Baals 'broken cisterns, that can hold no water' (Jeremiah 2^{13}). 'Your children have forsaken me, and have sworn by those who are no gods.' 'As many as your cities are your gods, O Judah' (Jeremiah 5^7, 2^{28}).

The kings of Israel and Judah are judged by the editors according to their attitude towards Baal worship. For example, Hezekiah 'did what was right in the eyes of the Lord' because 'he removed the high places, and broke the pillars, and cut down the Asherah' (2 Kings 18$^{3,\ 4}$). His son Manasseh did what was evil, for 'he rebuilt the high places' and 'he erected altars for Baal, and made an Asherah' (2 Kings 21^3). 'The graven image of Asherah that he had made' he put into the Temple at Jerusalem (2 Kings 21^7). This particular Asherah would be a wooden pillar carved after the fashion of a totem-pole.

In 621 B.C. King Josiah promoted a religious reform. In the course of it the vessels made for Baal and the Asherah were removed from the Temple, the idolatrous priests were deposed, and the houses of Temple prostitutes destroyed (2 Kings 23$^{4-14}$). All that was associated with fertility cult was purged.

94

There were four main factors that helped the Hebrews to pass beyond the fertility-cult stage of religion.

First, the book of Deuteronomy, on which Josiah had based his reform, required all sacrificial worship to take place only at the central sanctuary. This was taken to be the Temple at Jerusalem. Consequently the high places were closed down. People were permitted to kill animals for domestic use. This meant that they did not need a local high place in order to sacrifice their animals before eating (Deuteronomy 12^{1-16}, $16^{21, 22}$).

In the second place, the Exile brought about a conviction of God as the only Universal Creator. This meant that the Baals and Ashtaroth did not exist. Although this belief in only one God had been growing for some time, it was the shock of the Exile that made it explicit.

Thirdly, the Exile removed many of the Hebrews from contact with the Baals of Canaan and the temptation to acknowledge them. There were, of course, gods in Babylon where the Hebrews were in exile, but the Hebrews were living in a separate community, keeping themselves strictly apart from Babylonian contact, and looking forward to a return to Palestine – at least the keen devout Jews were. Many, on the other hand, settled in Babylon, and possibly were led astray by the gods.

Fourthly, during the Exile, something else had to be substituted for sacrificial worship. There came into being worship which consisted of readings from the Law and the Prophets, and the singing of psalms – later known as synagogue worship. Fertility cult was thus finally on the way out. After the Exile marriage with foreigners was condemned as a precaution against its revival.

10. The After-Life

No subject has proved more fascinating to the human race than the possibility of an after-life. Indeed the hope of such seems to have been so ingrained in mankind the world over, since the dawn of history, that many feel this to be strong evidence in its favour. Archaeologists discover more information concerning religious beliefs, and, in particular, the after-life, than anything else.

One has only to call to mind the many burial places of prehistoric man which have been unearthed, even the humblest containing some provisions for the use of the departed in some future existence, and, in more spectacular fashion, the tombs of the Egyptian pharaohs, crammed full of treasures for a dead king's use.

Mythology reveals many of the early beliefs concerning an after-life. Always it dealt with an 'underworld'. Often that had its own particular god. It was a place of no return. The story of Orpheus and Eurydice well illustrates the typical belief. The Egyptian Book of the Dead (finest known example dated 1500 B.C.) shows belief in a judgment of the soul when it appeared before Osiris and forty-two other judges. The book was placed in the coffin, and contained the sort of questionnaire which the soul would be required to answer.

The Babylonians believed the underworld to be a large hollow mountain, wherein everyone and everything was covered with dust. The poem known as the 'Desert of Ishtar' describes even the food as dust.

For some people, belief in an after-life assumed a positive existence for the soul; for others there was belief in a mere survival, the soul being only a 'shade'. Some burial customs removed the body to a cemetery away from the community, lest perhaps the dead person should, unsettled, or maliciously, haunt the survivors, or so that he might belong to the new community of his own kind. Others buried the dead near to his home or family, so that his spirit could still be among them.

The myths explaining the winter season of the year involve the idea of a god dying and rising again. The mother goddess of the earth mourns during the winter season, together with all Nature, because her child (or lover) is spending some months of the year in the underworld, and is therefore temporarily dead. His (or her) return to earth in the spring was a time of great rejoicing (see page 83).

Official Hebrew belief

Even in the first century A.D. official Judaism did not believe in an active after-life. The Sadducees were the ruling aristocracy (the High Priest was one of their number) and their distinctive belief was that there was no real after-life. 'For the Sadducees say that there is no resurrection, nor angel, nor spirit; but the Pharisees acknowledge them all' (Acts 23⁸). On this particular occasion St. Paul, a prisoner, managed to set the two parties arguing with each other by saying, 'With respect to the hope and the resurrection of the dead I am on trial' (Acts 23⁶). In this way he gained the sympathy of the Pharisees.

It was the same matter which led to the first arrests among the Apostles. Peter and John, having healed a lame man at the Beautiful Gate, were explaining the miracle to the crowd when 'the Sadducees came upon them, annoyed because they were teaching the people and proclaiming in Jesus the resurrection from the dead' (Acts 4¹, ²). Thus it was not so much blame for the death of Jesus, as the preaching of his Resurrection, and a resultant resurrection for his followers, which was so offensive to the chief priests and Sadducees.

It was the Sadducees who brought to Jesus the question concerning the woman married in turn to seven brothers (Mark 12¹⁸⁻²⁷). They wanted to know: 'In the resurrection whose wife will she be?' Such a situation was, no doubt, often seriously debated between them and the Pharisees. Here the foolishness of the situation was probably meant to discredit belief in after-life.

Hebrew belief in general

The Sadducean belief, or lack of it, did not represent the view of the great majority of Jews. The Pharisees, though not so powerful politically as the Sadducees, were far more numerous and spiritually influential. They did believe in an after-life. And it was during the time of the rise of the Pharisees, in the late post-exilic period, that an after-life really became a positive belief for Jews.

Pre-exilic belief

Hebrew religion was very much a religion for this world only. God's rewards to the righteous had to be given in this life, there being, it was believed, no other over which he had any control. Thus a long and prosperous life was regarded as a sign of God's favour. Added to the Fifth Commandment, as a reason for honouring parents, are the words: 'that your days may be long in the land which the Lord your God gives you' (Exodus 20¹²).

The Hebrew idea of the underworld was similar to that of the Babylonians. There was a great hollow beneath the ground called *Sheol*, 'hollow'. It corresponded to the Greek Hades. In English *Sheol* is variously translated as 'grave', 'pit', 'depth' and 'hell'. This is the origin of the imagery, which, continued through centuries, lingers today of hell as being 'down' and 'below'.

Sheol or hell was a place for the departed. It had no necessary connection with torment and punishment. Such ideas tended to develop in Christian times.

The dreadful thing about Sheol, for the devout Hebrew, was the thought that therein he was separated from God. Before the Exile, Yahweh's kingdom was not thought to extend beyond Hebrew territory, therefore Sheol was outside his control. It was not until the Hebrews reached a belief in Yahweh as the Universal Creator that an idea of the departed as being still with God could begin. In Hebrew belief there was no god of the underworld. The book of Job presents Satan, the Adversary, as 'going to and fro on the earth' (Job 1⁷) and as having a place in the court of heaven.

The gloom of Sheol pervades the words of Jacob when he imagines Joseph his son to be dead: 'No, I shall go down to Sheol to my son, mourning' (Genesis 37³⁵). To the request of his sons that Benjamin be allowed to go with them to Egypt, he says: 'You would bring down my grey hairs with sorrow to Sheol' (Genesis 42³⁸, 44²⁹, ³¹).

The idea of being 'swallowed up' into the underworld is to be found in mythology and, in the Old Testament, in the story of Korah's rebellion. 'The ground under them split asunder; and the earth opened its mouth and swallowed them up, with their households and all the men that belonged to Korah and all their goods. So they and all that belonged to them went down alive into Sheol; and the earth closed over them' (Numbers 16³⁰⁻³⁴).

The same idea is expressed in Isaiah 5¹⁴. 'Therefore Sheol has enlarged its appetite and opened its mouth beyond measure, and the nobility of Jerusalem and her multitude go down.'

There is perhaps a glimpse of the idea of Yahweh's having some power over Sheol in the words of Isaiah to King Ahaz: 'Ask a sign of the Lord your God; let it be deep as Sheol or high as heaven' (Isaiah 7¹⁰). By the time of Isaiah the extent of Yahweh's sovereignty was rapidly increasing in the minds of the prophets (Amos 5⁸⁻⁹, Isaiah 6³).

Isaiah believed Yahweh to have control over the destinies of other nations, and the whole earth was 'full of his glory'. King Ahaz was therefore given a very wide choice, from heaven to hell, in which to ask for some indication of divine intention.

Burial was regarded as very important by the Hebrews. It was a terrible thing for a body to remain unburied. Without burial there could be no hope of any after-life. Thus the inhabitants of Jabesh Gilead went by night to the Philistine city of Beth-shan to rescue the bodies of King Saul and his sons, which, after their defeat on Gilboa, were fastened to the city walls. The bones were given burial under a sacred tamarisk tree in Jabesh (1 Samuel 31$^{8-13}$).

The punishment of Jezebel was the more dreadful because, not only did she meet a violent death, but, when Jehu gave orders for her burial, it was too late. The dogs had left very little. She was therefore deprived of any after-life (2 Kings 9$^{34-37}$).

For the same reason Amos condemned the King of Moab 'because he burned to lime the bones of the King of Edom' (Amos 2^{1}).

Abraham bought the cave of Machpelah as a sepulchre for his family (Genesis 23). Samuel was buried in his own house at Ramah (1 Samuel 25^{1}). Deborah, Rebekah's nurse, was buried under a sacred oak (Genesis 35^{8}), and Rachel's grave was marked by a pillar (Genesis 35$^{19, 20}$). The familiar phrase used in the books of Kings, to end the reign of a king, is that he 'slept with his fathers, and was buried with his fathers'. Thus in death the family was reunited (2 Kings 15^{38}, 16^{20}).

The practice of Levirate marriage (Deuteronomy 25$^{5-10}$) arose because of the uncertainty about survival after death. There was a belief that a man's survival might last only so long as his name was remembered by his descendants. This sort of belief lies behind ancestor worship. Also there was the idea that a man's spirit lived on in his sons. It was therefore a misfortune if a man died childless, for then there was no one to perpetuate his name.

The Hebrew Law consequently made it a matter of obligation for a dead man's brother, or male next of kin, to have a son by the widow. This son 'shall succeed to the name of his brother who is dead, that his name may not be blotted out of Israel' (Deuteronomy 25^{6}).

The story of Ruth is an excellent illustration of this way of thinking. Though the book of Ruth is post-exilic, and written for a different purpose, it is set in the time of the Judges. Ruth is commended, not merely for her devotion to her mother-in-law, Naomi, but also because, by returning with Naomi to Bethlehem, she could meet her dead husband's people and find his next of kin. It was her devotion to her dead husband which caused her to meet Boaz. He was not in fact the immediate next of kin, but wanted nevertheless to accept that responsibility (Ruth 3$^{9-13}$, 4$^{1-10}$).

Although in many ways the Hebrews were so much more spiritually advanced than other peoples, they were particularly reserved by comparison in speculation about survival after death. This may have been because it was so prominent in the religions of surrounding peoples, whose practices they regarded as corrupt, and whose 'abominations' were not to be imitated, and also because (as previously stated) until the Exile they scarcely thought of the other world as being under Yahweh's jurisdiction.

The Deuteronomic Reform, 621 B.C., promoted by King Josiah, banned all those who practised necromancy (2 Kings 23[24]; Deuteronomy 18[9-12]). An interesting incident in the life of King Saul is evidence of the existence in Israel of spiritualism (1 Samuel 28).

Saul, anxious to know the outcome of his coming conflict with the Philistines, and failing to get any message through the approved oracles, consulted a medium. In the course of a séance she claimed to see the spirit of Samuel, who spoke through her to Saul: '. . . tomorrow you and your sons shall be with me . . .'

The story, which precedes the Deuteronomic Reform by 400 years, states that Saul had banned mediums and wizards, and that the woman was afraid to help Saul because of this (1 Samuel 28[3]). It is by no means certain, however, that this was so, for the editors of much Old Testament history were so influenced by the Deuteronomic laws that they frequently back-dated its ideals to an earlier age.

There was evidently no difficulty in finding a medium for Saul, despite his alleged ban (1 Samuel 28[7]). Saul's disguise was perhaps but the natural wish of a king to travel incognito, but it may have been adopted for particular reasons. He may have been anxious to hide from others his fears about the battle. He may have wished not to influence the medium (though she did in fact guess his identity). He may have been afraid of being recognized by the spirits, and particularly by Samuel who had rejected him (1 Samuel 15[35]).

Post-exilic belief

During the first centuries of the post-exilic period popular belief progressed very little. Now that belief in God as the Universal Creator had been reached, the way was open to advance; but, even so, the belief of a few theologians would not immediately become the common faith of the people.

Still the tragedy of death is expressed, as in Psalm 88[3-12]: 'I am reckoned among those who go down to the Pit. . . . Are thy wonders known in the darkness, or thy saving help in the land of forgetfulness?'

The same hopelessness is to be found in the poem put into the mouth of Hezekiah, King of Judah, thanking God for his recovery: 'For Sheol cannot thank thee, death cannot praise thee; those who go down to the pit cannot hope for thy faithfulness. The living, the living, he thanks thee, as I do this day' (Isaiah 38[18-19]).

Nevertheless the writer of Isaiah 14[9, 10] imagines the Shades greeting the King of Babylon, a newcomer in the underworld: 'Sheol beneath is stirred up to meet you when you come, it rouses the shades to greet you, all who were leaders of the earth; it raises from their thrones all who were kings of the nations. All of them will speak and say to you: "You too have become as weak as we! You have become like us!" '

These words, probably written during the Exile (as was Ezekiel 32[17-32]), suggest a certain animation on the part of the Shades, who are able to recognize and speak to the newcomer. Not only has he disturbed the world, now he disturbs them. Eminent people, it seems, could be distinguished from others even by the dead. Those who had been kings still sat on thrones, a privilege to be denied the King of Babylon as a punishment.

One of the most remarkable thinkers of the Old Testament was the unknown prophet of the Exile responsible for the messianic ideas unfolded in the four Servant Songs. It is perhaps not surprising that such a writer, when describing the Suffering Servant of Yahweh, should anticipate for him a life after death. After his death on behalf of his people the Servant would continue God's work (Isaiah 52[13]-53). But then the Servant was no ordinary person; nor is it certain whether the writer was describing the Hebrew nation or an individual as God's servant.

A belief that God rewarded the righteous with a long and prosperous earthly life did not always seem to fit the facts. The wicked were seen to prosper, and the good frequently suffered. If God did not reward or punish in this life, then where? This thought, together with that of the universal sovereignty of God, gradually led to a more positive belief in an after-life.

However, it is really not until the last four hundred years of Old Testament history that any glimpse of real progress appears. About 400 B.C. the story of Job was written as an attempt to deal with the problem of innocent suffering. Suffering in this life was believed to be God's punishment on the wicked. Yet Job could not recall that he was in any way guilty of offence.

For the most part the writer holds the traditional belief in Sheol, as in Job's lament that he did not die at birth: 'There the wicked cease from troubling, and the weary are at rest. There the prisoners are at ease together; they hear not the voice of the taskmaster. The small and the great are there, and the slave is free from his master' (Job 3[17-19]).

Unfortunately, the words most familiar and most often quoted from

101

the book of Job, as indicating a definite belief in an after-life with God (Job 19$^{25, 26}$), are far from expressing any certainty. All they indicate is perhaps a very faint possibility of survival. Job in his suffering is sure that God will redeem or vindicate him before his accusers. 'I shall see God,' he cries, but it is not at all clear whether he means in this life 'upon the earth', while he is still in the flesh, or after death, when he will be, he says, 'without my flesh'. Job, perhaps, is expressing no more than his confidence that God will have the last say.

Although the book of Job offered little hope of future reward (the book ends with a long and even more prosperous life than before as a reward for Job's faithfulness) another fourth-century writing did give more certainty. 'Thy dead shall live, their bodies shall rise. O dwellers in the dust, awake and sing for joy! For thy dew is a dew of light, and on the land of the shades thou wilt let it fall' (Isaiah 26^{19}).

These words are part of a poem in which Israel is expressing the hope of resurrection for her faithful dead, but not the dead of her enemies (Isaiah 26^{14}). The writer seems to be quite confident that this will happen. Slowly is dawning the realization that God's rewards, God's purposes, God's vindication of the faithful, whether of the individual or of the nation, may not, as once was thought, take place in this life.

It is not, however, until about 180 B.C. that this hope is taken up again in the book of Daniel (12^2): 'And many of those who sleep in the dust of the earth shall awake, some to everlasting life, and some to shame and everlasting contempt.'

The story is told in the Second Book of the Maccabees of a woman who saw her seven sons die as martyrs for their faith. She was certain that the lives that they were giving for God would in some way be restored to them: 'The Creator of the world, who shaped the beginning of man and devised the origin of all things, will in his mercy give life and breath back to you again, since you now forget yourselves for the sake of his laws' (2 Maccabees 7^{23}).

Her martyr sons shared her confidence, one saying as he died, 'You accursed wretch, you dismiss us from this present life, but the King of the universe will raise us up to an everlasting renewal of life, because we have died for his laws' (2 Maccabees 7^9). The last of the seven brothers to die said, 'our brothers after enduring a brief suffering have drunk of everflowing life under God's covenant' (2 Maccabees 7^{36}). The third to die even said that he expected to receive again his severed hands and threatened tongue (2 Maccabees 7$^{10, 11}$).

By the time another book of the Apocrypha was written (the Wisdom of Solomon) at the most a century before the birth of Jesus, hope in an after-life, in which God would reward the righteous, was expressed with glowing certainty.

In the first four chapters of this book the writer rebukes the 'eat, drink and be merry, for tomorrow we die' attitude of the ungodly, who falsely believe that this short life is all. He asserts that 'righteousness is immortal' (1^{15}), that 'God created man for incorruption, and made him in the image of his own eternity' (2^{23}), and that 'God did not make death' (1^{13}).

The author completely rejects the old idea that length of life is any indication of righteousness, for the good may die young (4^{7-14}). He sums up his belief in what have become well known words: 'The souls of the righteous are in the hand of God, and no torment will ever touch them' (3^1).

Two psalms express the highest form of belief in an after-life found in the Old Testament. The first (Psalm 139^{7-10}) affirms the universal sovereignty and omniscience of God, which includes the realm of the departed.

> Whither shall I go from thy Spirit?
>   Or whither shall I flee from thy presence?
> If I ascend to heaven, thou art there!
>   If I make my bed in Sheol, thou art there!
> If I take the wings of the morning
>   and dwell in the uttermost parts of the sea,
> even there shall thy hand lead me,
>   and thy right hand shall hold me.

The second (Psalm 73^{24-26}) could have been written by a Christian poet, so close is it to New Testament teaching.

> Thou dost guide me with thy counsel,
>   and afterward thou wilt receive me to glory.
> Whom have I in heaven but thee?
>   And there is nothing upon earth that I desire besides thee.
> My flesh and my heart may fail,
>   but God is the strength of my heart and my portion for ever.

11. Hebrew Festivals

The earliest Decalogue of the Pentateuch (source J) required Hebrew males to observe three festivals. 'Three times in the year shall all your males appear before the Lord God, the God of Israel' (Exodus 34²³). So too did the Book of the Covenant, source E (Exodus 23¹⁴⁻¹⁷). They were the pastoral and agricultural festivals of Passover and Unleavened Bread; the feast of Weeks or First Fruits, better known as Pentecost; the feast of Ingathering or Tabernacles (Exodus 34¹⁸⁻²⁶).

Other festivals were added later, but the original three reflect the early life of the Hebrew community. Agricultural peoples, the world over, have seen special religious significance in the corn harvest, especially in the first gathered and the last sheaf. Their ancient observances still survive in many local customs.

The Hebrews came to acknowledge their God as the life force of their harvest. After the Exile in Babylon the prophet Haggai saw the poor crops and harvest as a direct result of the failure of the Hebrews to rebuild God's Temple. 'Because of my house that lies in ruins . . . the earth has witheld its produce' (Haggai 1⁹, ¹⁰).

Hebrew festivals, however, became much more important than agricultural celebrations. They gained new significance as reminders of Yahweh's great achievements in their history: they marked historical events. Thus the Passover and the feast of Unleavened Bread commemorated the hasty Exodus from Egypt; Pentecost commemorated the lawgiving on Mount Sinai; and Tabernacles was a reminder of the tent-dwelling days of wandering in the wilderness.

The Passover and Unleavened Bread (14th Nisan and 15th–21st Nisan or Abib – March or April)

The Passover was originally a festival of thanksgiving for new-born lambs. It was an ancient belief that first fruits of humans, animals and crops were the special property of the deity. Human sacrifice of the firstborn was quickly outgrown by the Hebrews (see p. 88), and the priests accepted the payment of five shekels by way of redemption (Numbers 18¹⁵, ¹⁶; source P).

When Moses and Aaron asked the Pharaoh's permission for the Hebrews to leave Egypt, this reason was given: 'Thus says the Lord, the God of Israel, "Let my people go, that they may hold a feast to me in the wilderness." ' (Exodus 5¹.) It may well have been the Passover that they wished to keep, for this festival coincided with the escape (Exodus 12²¹).

Whether or not that was so, the Passover gained deeper meaning as the commemoration of the escape, regarded by Jews as the supreme intervention by Yahweh in their history. Without it there would have been no nation.

Exodus 12 gives the account of the Passover that the Hebrews were observing in Egypt when news of the Pharaoh's permission to leave reached them. Every future Passover recalled that dramatic escape. Much of Exodus 12 comes from the priestly writers (source P) who describe the event as it had come to be commemorated over the centuries, with prescribed rules and ceremonial (Exodus 12¹⁻²⁰, ²⁸, ³⁷, ⁴⁰⁻⁵¹). But the heart of the story is from the early source J.

The Passover was held in the first month of the year, Abib or Nisan (about our March). On the tenth day each family or household took a male lamb, a year old and without blemish, and kept it apart until the fourteenth day, to make sure that it was in fact free from defects. There was, of course, no time for such delay on that last night in Egypt (Exodus 12²¹, ²²). Then each family slew its own lamb, and sprinkled the blood, the symbol of life, on to the lintels and door posts of the houses.

The religious reform instituted by King Josiah in 621 B.C. was marked by a solemn celebration of the Passover according to the rules laid down in Deuteronomy 16¹⁻⁸ (2 Kings 23²¹⁻²³). These rules specified that the Passover might be observed only within the boundaries of Jerusalem, and that the lambs should be sacrificed 'at the place which the Lord your God will choose, to make his name dwell in it', i.e. the Temple.

It is not clear whether the early Passover sacrifices were boiled or roasted. Boiling was the usual method of preparing a sacrificial meal. The two priest sons of Eli were regarded as sinners because they would not accept boiled meat as their dues, insisting instead upon their portion being roasted (1 Samuel 2¹²⁻¹⁷). The earliest account of the Exodus or Egyptian Passover (Exodus 12²¹⁻²⁷, ²⁹⁻³⁴: source J) does not specify how the meat was to be prepared, but the Deuteronomic laws state that it should be boiled (Deuteronomy 16⁷; cf. A.V. roast, and R.V. roast or boil).

The instruction to roast the Passover lamb appears in the later priestly account (Exodus 12⁸, ⁹) and the same priestly source insisted that no bone of the sacrifice should be broken (Exodus 12⁴⁶). Boiling involved cutting an animal into pieces. Roasting was a way of preparing the sacrifice whole, for thus it came to symbolize the unity of Israel.

The meal or *seder*, as it is called, was eaten during the evening following 14th Nisan, with the participants dressed ready as for a journey. This was a reminder of that night in Egypt when the Hebrews were told to be ready to leave at any time. So also, said the Rabbi Gamaliel, were the bitter herbs a reminder of the bitterness of slavery. The youngest member of the family had to ask: 'What do you mean by this service?' The answer given by the head of the family was: 'It is the sacrifice of the Lord's passover. . . .' (Exodus 12²⁶, ²⁷). At intervals portions of the Hallel (Psalms 113–118) were sung.

All the three sources agree that the remains of the sacrifice should be burnt before daybreak (Exodus 34²⁵J; Deuteronomy 16⁴D; Exodus 12¹⁰P). There is some thought that this may have been a survival from the days of moon worship, when traces of sacrifices to the moon had to be removed before sunrise. The Passover always came at the time of full-moon. A later reason was that which ordered the disposal of all sacrificial remains by fire, to avoid the possibility of contamination by holiness. The use of an animal for sacrifice involved its becoming holy (see p. 90).

A second Passover could be held a month later for those unable to keep the first.

On the day following the Passover meal started the feast of Unleavened Bread, observed for seven days from Nisan 15th–21st. This feast became a reminder of the actual escape from Egypt, when such was the haste that there was no time for the bread to rise in the usual way (Exodus 12³⁹). So closely connected were the two feasts that the Passover and Unleavened Bread became alternative names for the eight days Nisan 14th–21st, and Nisan 14th could be referred to as the first day of Unleavened Bread as well as being the day when the Passover lambs were sacrificed (Mark 14¹²).

The references in the book of Exodus to the feast of Unleavened Bread come from the early source J, both in the Decalogue (34¹⁸) and in the Passover account (12³⁹). In very early times, however, the two feasts of Passover and Unleavened Bread were quite distinct. It was the historical meaning given to them which linked them.

The Passover, as has been seen, was an early pastoral feast, and the feast of Unleavened Bread was originally an agricultural one concerning the yeast cycle. After each baking of bread a small portion of dough was kept aside to leaven the next baking. Once a year this cycle was broken, and unleavened bread was eaten during the week of the feast to ensure that no yeast remained. Then, with the fresh barley crop, a new yeast cycle could begin.

The fermentation involved in the producing of yeast caused the Jews to regard it as unclean. Jesus used it as a symbol of corrupting influences when he warned his disciples to: 'Take heed, beware of the leaven of the Pharisees and the leaven of Herod' (Mark 8[15]).

Present-day observance of the Passover involves no roasting of a whole lamb. Instead, roasted eggs and joints of lamb act as symbols of new life, and a reminder of the ancient Passover observance before the destruction of the Temple in A.D. 70. The herbs and unleavened bread can still be used. So too can the special cup of wine which was poured out for Elijah, for it was believed that he would return as a forerunner of the Messiah.

References:
J. Exodus 12[21-27, 29-34, 37b-39], 34[18, 25]
E. Exodus 12[35-36], 23[15]
D. Deuteronomy 16[1-8]
P. Exodus 12[1-20, 28, 37a, 40-51]; Leviticus 23[5-8]; Numbers 28[16-25]

Pentecost (6th Sivan – June early summer)

This harvest festival was alternatively called the feast of First Fruits because it marked the beginning of the wheat harvest, and the feast of Weeks because it was held seven weeks, or fifty days 'from the time you first put the sickle to the standing grain' (Leviticus 23[15, 16]; Deuteronomy 16[9]). This meant seven weeks from the feast of Unleavened Bread, which marked the beginning of the barley harvest. The word Pentecost comes from the Greek word for fiftieth.

A distinctive feature of the festival was the solemn waving of two leavened loaves, baked from the new wheat, as an acknowledgment to God as the giver (Leviticus 23[17-20]).

The early command to keep the feast appears in the Decalogue of Exodus 34[22]: source J.

The law of Deuteronomy bade the Hebrews, while rejoicing because of the harvest, to recall the slavery of their ancestors, and to be doubly grateful to God, for a harvest festival is a privilege of free people (Deuteronomy 16[12], 26[5-11]). Thus this festival of agricultural origin acquired an historical association.

Very much later Pentecost became also a commemoration of the Covenant-making at Mount Sinai.

References:
J. Exodus 34[22]
E. Exodus 23[16, 19]
D. Deuteronomy 16[9-12], 26[2-11]
P. Leviticus 23[15-21]; Numbers 28[26-31]

Tabernacles (15th–21st Tishri or Ethanim – October, autumn)

The feast of Tabernacles is alternatively known as the feast of In-gathering or the feast of Booths. It was held in the seventh month of the Hebrew year, and was the last of the three agricultural festivals. It was the autumn harvest festival, and denoted the completion of the agricultural year. Unleavened Bread and Pentecost were thanksgivings for the grain crop, but Tabernacles included the fruit and wine crops also.

The early command to keep the feast appears in the Decalogue of Exodus 34²² (source J), and in the Book of the Covenant, Exodus 23¹⁶ (source E). The law of Deuteronomy specified that the feast should be observed for seven days.

The priestly laws instructed people to 'take on the first day the fruit of goodly trees, branches of palm trees, and boughs of leafy trees, and willows of the brook; and you shall rejoice before the Lord your God seven days' (Leviticus 23⁴⁰). Thus worshippers at the Temple during the days of the feast carried in their hands sprays of myrtle, palm, and willow, together with grapes and citrons. These were also used for decoration, in much the same way as holly is now used at Christmas.

The distinctive features of the festival that give it its name also appear in the priestly law: 'You shall dwell in booths for seven days; all that are native in Israel shall dwell in booths, that your generations may know that I made the people of Israel dwell in booths when I brought them out of the land of Egypt' (Leviticus 23⁴², ⁴³). Thus yet another festival of agricultural origin became an historical reminder of Yahweh's great act of deliverance from Egypt, without which there would have been no nation.

The booths (Hebrew *succoth*, Latin *tabernacles*) were a reminder of the temporary dwellings of the wilderness period. During the seven days of the feast everyone camped out in them. Women and infants were exempt from this, so too were the sick and those attending them. People who came to Jerusalem for the feast lived in booths which they erected on the neighbouring hillsides. The booths were made of boughs of trees.

The present day custom is for Jews to erect a booth in their gardens or homes, and a special one, decorated with fruit, flowers and vegetables, is erected at the synagogue.

The seven days of the feast involved the daily offering of many sacrifices. One kid goat was offered daily as a sin offering, together with burnt offerings of lambs, rams and bullocks, totalling 182 animals at the end of the feast. With each burnt offering there was also a meat and drink offering.

Daily, except on the Sabbath, a priest went in procession from the Temple to the Pool of Siloam, and filled a gold pitcher with water. The procession returned to the Temple by way of the Water Gate, and arrived at the time when the morning sacrifices were about to be offered. The priest solemnly poured out the water for all to see, into a silver basin at the left of the altar.

The pouring out of water had a double symbolism, for it was a reminder that the winter season of rain was about to start, and also that God, who had provided water in the wilderness, would not fail to provide it again. It was also an illustration of the outpouring of God's Spirit. The ceremony is thought to have been the moment mentioned in John 7[2, 37].

After the pouring out of the water, the wine of the drink offerings was poured into a second silver bowl. At this point the psalms known as the Hallel were sung (Psalms 113–118), *Hallelujah* meaning 'Praise ye the Lord'. During the singing of Psalm 118 the people waved their branches of myrtle, palm and willow, particularly during verse 25 at the words 'save us' (in Hebrew *hosannah*). For this reason the branches themselves were sometimes known as hosannahs.

It was the Hallel psalms which were used to welcome pilgrims to Jerusalem, and verses 25 and 26 of Psalm 118 which were particularly applied to Jesus, when he rode into the city (Mark 11[8–10]). The waving of branches was, as has been noted, associated with this psalm at the feast of Tabernacles.

Another attractive feature of the Temple celebrations was the ceremonial lighting of four great candelabra. This took place in the Court of the Women on the first evening of the feast. The light from the candelabra lit up the surrounding city during the nights of the feast. The Temple was God's dwelling place, and this light was a sign of his glory shining into the darkness of the world around. It was the hope of the prophets that the Temple would be the spiritual centre of the world, and that from it God's law would go forth (Isaiah 2[2–5]; Micah 4[1–4]).

As with the pouring of the water, so this ceremony of lighting the candelabra is thought to have been the moment mentioned in John 8[12].

The idea of the Glory of God was important to the Hebrews. They spoke of it as the 'Shechinah', and this denoted the actual presence of God. It was the Shechinah that descended upon the Ark of the Covenant when Solomon dedicated the first Temple. This occurred at the feast of Tabernacles. When the Ark was brought into the Temple 'the glory of the Lord filled the house of the Lord' (1 Kings 8[2, 10, 11]).

Jewish tradition said that the pillar of cloud and fire which led the Hebrews through the wilderness first appeared on the 15th Tishri. On that day also it was said that Moses gave the people instructions to build

109

the Tabernacle. So once again a Jewish ceremony linked the present with the past and foreshadowed the future.

References:
J. Exodus 34[22]
E. Exodus 23[16b]
D. Deuteronomy 16[13-16]
P. Leviticus 23[34-43]; Numbers 29[12-39]

The Day of Atonement (10th Tishri – October)

The Day of Atonement (Hebrew *Yom Kippur*) is the most solemn day in the Jewish year. It takes place five days before the feast of Tabernacles, and is a day of national penitence before the day of national rejoicing.

The commands to observe the day appear only in the priestly writings. These are also the only Old Testament references to it. This suggests, though by no means conclusively, that the Day of Atonement was an observance which came into being, or perhaps into prominence, after the Exile.

Before the Exile the prophets had constantly urged the nation to repent, for they could see disaster ahead. The Exile was indeed shock treatment for the Hebrews, and led to more spiritual maturity. Now the nation realized that it had sinned, and that atonement was needed in order to restore its covenant relationship with God.

There were three distinctive features that marked the observance of the Day of Atonement. First, it was the only day of the year when the High Priest entered the innermost shrine of the Temple, the Holy of Holies or the Most Holy Place, the actual presence of God.

Second, the High Priest officiated at all the sacrifices of the day, the regular daily morning and evening sacrifices, the festive sacrifices for the Day of Atonement itself (Numbers 29[7-11]), and the special sacrifices of atonement for sin.

Third, for the atonement sacrifices the High Priest changed from his golden robes into special simple white linen garments, similar to those of ordinary priests, but wearing a white, not a coloured, girdle. Thus simply clad in white, the symbol of purity, the High Priest led the nation in penitence. For all the other sacrifices of the day the High Priest wore his usual golden vestments.

Seven days before the Day of Atonement the High Priest took up residence in the Temple, and began a period of intense preparation and rehearsal.

The atonement sacrifices special to this day are described in Leviticus 16 as though they had indeed taken place in the time of Moses. The Day of Atonement began early with the High Priest changing from his ordinary garments into his golden vestments in order to offer the ordinary daily morning sacrifices. These completed, he washed, and changed into the linen garments for the atonement sacrifices.

The High Priest then took a bullock and placed it between the Temple porch and the altar, facing the sanctuary. The High Priest, facing towards the congregation, laid his hands upon the bullock's head, and solemnly confessed that he and his household had sinned.

Next he took two goats and cast lots to determine which goat was for the Lord (i.e. to be sacrificed) and which goat was to be driven out into the wilderness bearing away the nation's sins. This latter, the 'scapegoat', was said to be for Azazel, probably a demon spirit of the wilderness akin to Satan, and was placed facing the people.

The High Priest then returned to the bullock. Again he laid his hands upon it and confessed the sins of himself, his household and the priesthood. After this he killed the bullock, and its blood was collected in a vessel.

Taking a censer and incense he entered the Holy of Holies, now empty and dark and filled with smoke. Once, in the days of Solomon's Temple, the Holy of Holies had contained the Ark of the Covenant, but that was lost, and so the post-exilic Temple, and later Herod's Temple, had nothing in the Holy of Holies. The High Priest left his censer smoking inside the Holy of Holies while he went out to fetch the blood of the bullock. This he sprinkled in the Holy of Holies, imagining the Ark still to be there.

Again the High Priest emerged. He set down the bowl of bullock's blood and killed the goat. Again he entered the Holy of Holies to sprinkle the goat's blood in the same way as before. Coming out yet again he sprinkled blood from both bullock and goat around the curtained entrance to the Holy of Holies. Then, mixing the blood together, he sprinkled the four horns or corners of the altar of incense and seven times sprinkled its top. The remaining blood he poured out at the base of the altar of burnt offering.

All this he had to do without getting his garments stained. The blood sprinkling indicated the cleansing not only of priests and people, but also of the Temple itself, which they, as sinners, had used.

Finally the High Priest put both his hands upon the head of the scapegoat and entreated God to forgive the sins of his people. Turning to the people the High Priest assured them that they would be cleansed. The goat, bearing the nation's sins, was led out through Solomon's porch. A relay of men accompanied the goat to the wilderness, and then signalled its arrival there back to the Temple. Meanwhile the carcases of the bullock and the other goat were taken outside the city and burned.

111

After Scripture readings and prayers the atonement observances were complete. The High Priest washed and resumed his golden vestments for the offering of the festive burnt offerings, followed by the ordinary evening sacrifice. After further washing he again put on his linen garments in order to go back into the Holy of Holies and remove the censer. Changing back once more into his vestments he offered the evening incense.

His duties finished he put on his ordinary garments and went to his home.

References:
P. Exodus 30[10]; Leviticus 16, 23[24-32]; Numbers 29[7-11]; cf. Epistle to the Hebrews, chapters 8 and 9 etc.

New Year's Day (Rosh Hoshanah, 'The feast of Trumpets – 1st Tishri)

In days before clocks and calendars marked the passing of time, the sun and moon provided natural means of doing so (see pp. 19 and 114). The moon has given us the months of the year. Hebrew religion had roots in moon worship. So, before this was forbidden or outgrown, the appearance of a new moon was celebrated, for it marked the beginning of another month, which had to be dedicated to the moon god (Psalm 81[3]; Isaiah 1[13, 14], 66[23]; Hosea 2[11]).

It was important to be precise about the moment when a new month began, because the great festivals had to be reckoned from New Moon Day. It could not be left for everyone to decide for himself. Among the Hebrews the custom grew up whereby certain people were appointed as witnesses, and they reported to the Council when they had actually seen the new moon. Astronomical calculations were not allowed.

When the Council proclaimed: 'It is sanctified', the priests blew the trumpets proclaiming a new month, which began at that point. Special sacrifices were offered, in addition to the statutory daily ones, to mark the new moon day. They now had nothing to do with moon worship, for they were offered to God with the intention of consecrating the new month to him (Numbers 28[11-15]).

The blowing of trumpets has from ancient times been a means of calling people together, calling soldiers to battle, and sounding an alarm. The military still make use of them. The blowing of trumpets and horns in distinctive manners was thus the means of announcing the beginning of a new month, and the commencement of the various feasts and fasts of the Hebrew year (Numbers 10[1-10]).

The first month of the agricultural year was that of Abib or Nisan, the month of the Passover (Exodus 12[2]; Deuteronomy 16[1]). Every seventh day was sacred and was kept as a Sabbath, and the seventh or sabbatical month was likewise regarded as special. It was the month of Tishri, the month of the Day of Atonement, and of the feast of Tabernacles.

The New Moon Day that marked the beginning of the seventh month was known as the feast of Trumpets, for it was marked by trumpet blowing all day long (Leviticus 23$^{23-25}$; Numbers 29$^{1-6}$). It is also the Jewish New Year's Day, for it marks the beginning of the Jewish chronological year. Jewish tradition says that the world was created in the month of Tishri, and the Jewish calendar counts the years from this traditional date of creation. Also in the month of Tishri life began again for the nation after the Exile (Ezra 3$^{1-6}$).

New Year's Day is followed by the Day of Atonement on the tenth day. The intervening days have become known as the Ten Days of Penitence. The *shofar* is now sounded in the synagogue at the beginning and end of the Ten Days. The *shofar* is a long horn so called because it is turned up at the end. It is the traditional instrument for arousing enthusiasm.

References:
P. Exodus 12^2; Leviticus 23^{24}; Numbers 10$^{1-10}$, 28$^{11-15}$
Also Psalm 81^3; Isaiah 1$^{13, 14}$, 66^{23}; Ezekiel 46^1; Hosea 2^{11}, Amos 8^5

Feast of the Dedication (25th Chislev – December)

The feast of the Dedication (Hebrew *Hanukkah*) is also known as the feast of Lights. It was of late origin, being established in 164 B.C. by Judas Maccabaeus, the Jewish hero during the Syro-Greek period of domination.

At this time the Temple was defiled by King Antiochus IV, known as Antiochus Epiphanes, who rededicated it to Zeus (Daniel 11^{31}, 12^{11}; 1 Maccabees 1$^{41-64}$ – see also 2 Maccabees 6$^{1-12}$). The king bitterly persecuted the Jews, many of whom died as martyrs, in his attempt to stamp out Judaism.

When the Jews regained their independence, Judas Maccabaeus and his company set about cleansing and repairing the Temple. The defiled altar was removed and a new one built. On the 25th Chislev it was dedicated, and sacrifice to God was once again offered in his re-hallowed sanctuary (1 Maccabees 4$^{36-59}$; 2 Maccabees 10$^{1-9}$).

Thereafter the feast of the Dedication was to be held each year for eight days beginning on the 25th Chislev. 'They celebrated it for eight days with rejoicing, in the manner of the feast of booths. . . . Therefore bearing ivy-wreathed wands and beautiful branches and also fronds of palm, they offered hymns of thanksgiving' (2 Maccabees 10$^{6, 7}$). Thus the ceremonies of this festival came to resemble those of the great feast of Tabernacles; but at first the ivy-wreathed wands were possibly in

113

triumphant and even derisive imitation of the *thyrsi* recently seen in Festivals of Bacchus.

The people carried palm branches, the Hallel psalms were sung, and the Temple was illuminated to commemorate the relighting of the great golden lampstand (1 Maccabees 4⁵⁰). Candles and lamps were lit also in the homes of Jewish families. This gave the feast its alternative name of feast of Lights.

Feast of Purim (14th–15th Adar – March)

The feast was, and still is, a popular observance, but one not entirely approved by all Jews. Its origin was as late as the second century B.C., and so its observance is not mentioned in the Pentateuch. The story of its origin is to be found on page 70.

The word *purim* is said to mean lots, though this is by no means the certain meaning of the word. The lots were said to have been cast by enemies of the Jews in order to determine a day suitable for their massacre. The day became one of rejoicing at deliverance from all their enemies. The triumph of Judaism over all its enemies was typified in the story of Esther and Mordecai. The festival was observed locally in the synagogues.

The 13th Adar was observed as a fast, known as the Fast of Esther, unless it fell upon the Sabbath, or preparation for the Sabbath, in which case the fast took place on Thursday. On the evening beginning the 14th Adar the Roll of Esther, known as the Megillah (i.e. *the* Roll), was read in public. The reading was quite melodramatic, for the whole congregation joined in with appropriate cheers and boos at the mention of the Jewish hero Mordecai and heroine Esther, and the wicked Haman.

Apart from the preceding fast, and the reading of Esther, local custom decreed ways in which the feast might be further celebrated. These now include parties, carnivals and processions, general merry-making and dressing-up to portray the characters in the story (Esther 3⁷, 9²¹⁻²⁴).

The Sabbath

The Sabbath was not a Jewish invention, nor was it exclusive to Judaism, though the Sabbath as kept by the Jews did acquire its own characteristics as a day of worship and a day free from work.

Its origin lies probably in the moon worship widely practised in the Middle East well before the time of Abraham. The same origin gives us the month and the seven-day week.

Early communities doubtless found that a regular day off work was required for the well-being of all. In days when there were no calendars or regular man-made means of marking the passing of time, the observance of nature provided some help. The regular cycle of four seasons would thus give a year, and the changing aspects of the moon would help the further sub-division of the year.

The moon was a natural object of worship. People noted that there was a new moon every twenty-eight days, and that twelve or thirteen months ('moonths') made a year. The twenty-eight days were further divided according to the four phases of the moon, so giving four weeks of seven days.

For moon worshippers every seventh day became, not only the day off work, but a religious day as well. Abraham would be familiar with this sort of Sabbath. The week of six days of work, and the seventh day of rest and worship, was already a familiar pattern of life in his day.

Abraham himself was probably a moon worshipper when he lived in Ur of the Chaldees. One reason for the migration of his father's tribe from Ur to Haran (Genesis 11[31, 32]) may well have been the arrival of Hammurabi as king, and his desire to promote sun worship. In Haran there was a moon temple.

The Hebrews had no reason to alter the pattern of the seven-day week, even when Yahweh worship superseded that of the moon. New moons and sabbaths are frequently mentioned in the Old Testament, and the present Jewish calendar still retains ancient links with moon worship.

The prophet Hosea of the Northern Kingdom said in the name of God: 'I will put an end to all her mirth, her feasts, her new moons, her sabbaths' (Hosea 2[11]). Isaiah likewise in the south: 'Your new moons and your appointed feasts my soul hates' (Isaiah 1[13, 14]). The worship of the moon was later forbidden as a result of the Deuteronomic Reform in 621 B.C. (Deuteronomy 17[2-5]; 2 Kings 23[5]).

The command to keep the Sabbath appears in the Decalogue. The earliest Decalogue, gave no religious reason for keeping it. 'Six days you shall work, but on the seventh day you shall rest' (Exodus 34[21]). This reflects the origin of the Sabbath in man's need for a regular day off work.

The Decalogue of Deuteronomy 5 does give the Sabbath religious significance by speaking of the seventh day as 'a Sabbath to the Lord your God'. This version is insistent that the seventh day be a day of rest for all, servants as well as masters, and a day of thankful remembrance by the Hebrews that they were free to have a sabbath. Once they had been slaves in Egypt, and God had delivered them (Deuteronomy 5[12-15]).

The best known Decalogue, that of Exodus 20, is compiled from all the major sources of the Pentateuch. For the most part its Sabbath law resembles that of Deuteronomy, but with the omission of reference to slavery in Egypt. In its place the priestly editors of the Exile added

(Exodus 20[11]) a reference to their recently written parable of Creation (Genesis 1–2[4a]). This parable (see p. 62) was concerned to stress the truth that Yahweh was the Universal Creator – a truth which was the most important theological advance of the Exile.

The priests must have thought that this truth was more vital even than the Exodus. Thus the Decalogue shows the development of the Hebrew Sabbath from being a 'day of rest' only, to one marking recognition of Yahweh the Deliverer, and then to one marking recognition of Yahweh the Creator.

The name 'sabbath' comes from the Hebrew *shabath*, meaning to rest. It is similar to the Babylonian name of *shapattu*, for the festival of the full moon on the fourteenth of the month. On the seventh-day festivals of the moon it was considered unlucky to perform certain tasks.

It is easy enough to prohibit work but far more difficult to define it. The Hebrew Scribes or lawyers, in their zeal to emphasize the sanctity of the Sabbath, got very involved in this matter, and by New Testament times the day had become one of detailed regulations, tending to obscure the original sense of freedom.

Jesus summed up the whole history of the Sabbath, and the Scribes' attitude towards it, by saying, 'The Sabbath was made for man, not man for the Sabbath.' His disciples had been accused of working on the Sabbath because they had plucked ears of corn. This was technically reaping, and therefore work on the Sabbath (Mark 2[23–28]). Jesus' 'works' of healing were also regarded as contravening the Sabbath.

During the Exile the keeping of the Jewish Sabbath was one of the ways in which the Hebrews maintained their distinction from the Babylonians, in whose land they lived, even though the Babylonians also observed their seventh days. The Jewish Sabbath was similar in some respects to the Babylonian, but, by this time, had become very different from the seventh day observed by the heathens. Such was the Jewish devotion to their Sabbath that, during the Seleucid persecution of Jews, many died as martyrs rather than break the Sabbath observance.

The Jewish Sabbath falls on a Saturday. It is timed from sunset on Friday to sunset on Saturday. The first Christians were Jews, and so they observed the Sabbath in the customary way, but, in addition, they kept Sunday, the day of the Resurrection of Jesus, as a day of worship. Before long the Christian Church became predominantly Gentile, and after 313 A.D., when Christianity became the official religion of the Roman Empire, the Emperor Constantine decreed (321 A.D.) that Sunday should be a non-working day throughout the Empire.

And so, our established weekend of Saturday and Sunday owes its origin to two religions, Judaism and Christianity.

JEWISH CALENDAR

	MONTHS	FESTIVALS	ANCIENT ASSOCIATION	HEBREW COMMEMORATION
1st month	*Abib or Nisan* April 1st Day 14th Day 15th–21st Day	New Moon Day *Pesach* Passover Unleavened Bread	Worship of the new moon Full moon festival of new-born lambs Beginning of barley harvest: yeast cycle broken	Month consecrated to God God's deliverance of his people from Egyptian slavery The haste of the Exodus
3rd month	*Sivan* June 1st Day 6th Day	New Moon Day *Shabuoth* Pentecost or feast of Weeks	Beginning of wheat harvest	The Covenant and lawgiving at Sinai
7th month	*Tishri or Ethanim* October 1st Day 10th Day 15th–21st Day	New Moon Day *Rosh Hoshanah* or Trumpets *Yom Kippur* Day of Atonement *Succoth* Tabernacles, Booths, Ingathering	All new moons heralded by trumpets, marking a new month The great harvest festival	The sabbatical or 7th month – special celebrations to mark Civil New Year Penitence for national sin Wanderings in the wilderness
9th month	*Chislev* December 1st Day 25th Day	New Moon Day *Hanukkah* Dedication		New temple altar dedicated after Seleucid defilement
12th month	*Adar* March 1st Day 14th–15th Day	New Moon Day *Purim* Feast of Esther or Lots	Probably had its origin in Babylonian folklore	Triumph of Jewish nationalism

12. Israel's Worship

The majority of the regulations in the Old Testament concerning Israel's worship came from the exilic priestly source P, and some from the slightly earlier source D. These two later sources continue the style of the earlier Hebrew legislators, and put the laws in the form of commands given by God to Moses.

Thus, although the laws of D and P are much later than Moses, laws relating to the offering of sacrifice are put into the mouth of Moses, laws concerning the High Priest and the priesthood are directed to Aaron and his sons, and the scene of Hebrew worship is set in the Tabernacle, although the writers have the Temple in mind.

Most, though by no means all, of source P is to be found in the Pentateuch. In addition to the book of Leviticus, there are many portions in the book of (e.g. Exodus, chapters 25-31, 35-40) and in the book of Numbers (e.g. chapters 1-10^{28}, 17-19, 25^{6}-31, 33-36).

The Tabernacle

The first meeting place used by the Hebrews for worship was the Tabernacle, or portable tent, which Moses erected outside the camp during Israel's nomadic years in the wilderness. The Ark of the Covenant was kept in it, which meant that the Tabernacle was essentially God's residence, literally apart from the people (see p. 90).

Very little is known about the Tabernacle, for the only early mention of it is in Exodus 33$^{5-11}$ (source E). All the elaborate descriptions of the Tabernacle to be found in the Pentateuch come from the priestly writings of the Exile and after.

The priests looked upon the Tabernacle as the prototype of both the Temple that they had known before the Exile, and of the ideal Temple which they planned for the future. Their first Temple had existed for four hundred years, and many of its features were possibly assumed to have existed in the Tabernacle also.

When the Ark of the Covenant was brought into the land of Canaan it no longer rested in the Tabernacle. It was housed in a shrine at

Shiloh. There it remained until its capture by the Philistines. After its return it was kept in the house of Abinadab, and later in the house of Obed-edom. King David then brought it to Jerusalem, where another tent or tabernacle was waiting for it (2 Samuel 6³, ¹², ¹⁷; Psalm 132⁶⁻⁸). It is worth noting that 'it' in verse 6 of the Psalm refers to the Ark.

Solomon's Temple

Among Solomon's many building projects was that of building a Temple. It is not often referred to as a Temple, but as 'the house of the Lord' or 'the place which the Lord your God will choose, to make his name dwell there' (Deuteronomy 12⁵, ¹¹; 1 Kings 5, 6; Isaiah 2²). The building was regarded first and foremost as the actual dwelling place of God, now in the midst of his people. He came to take up residence when the Ark of the Covenant was brought into the Temple at its dedication (1 Kings 8⁶⁻¹³).

The Temple was not large, although it was said to be twice the size of the Tabernacle. At first it was more a chapel royal adjacent to the king's palace, but it was soon regarded as the national shrine. It was of Phoenician design and resembled contemporary temples in other lands. It consisted of an open courtyard which contained a covered hall or house. Part of the hall was set apart as a sanctuary or Holy of Holies. Inside this inner shrine the image of a god was kept, but in the Holy of Holies in their Temple the Hebrews kept the Ark of the Covenant.

Many believed that Jerusalem would never be captured by an enemy, because it contained the Lord's house, but four hundred years after Solomon built it, it was plundered, in 586 B.C., by the Babylonians, who carried away its treasures (2 Kings 24¹³), and destroyed the building by fire (2 Kings 25⁹, ¹³⁻¹⁷).

Zerubbabel's Temple

In 537 B.C., after fifty years of exile in Babylon, Cyrus, King of Persia, permitted those Jews who wished, to return to Jerusalem. 'Whoever is among you of all his people, may his God be with him, and let him go up to Jerusalem, which is in Judah, and rebuild the house of the Lord, the God of Israel....' (Ezra 1¹⁻⁴.)

It was only the more patriotic Jews who by this time wished to return. Many had settled down comfortably in Babylon, where some had been born. Moreover the growing realization that Yahweh was the God of the Universe, and not merely of Palestine, made a return not an essential act of faith.

However, a contingent led by Sheshbazzar did return, and brought

119

with it the Temple treasures, as well as many gifts (Ezra 1⁵⁻⁹). These people were followed by another party led by Zerubbabel and Jeshua, who rebuilt the altar within the Temple ruins, so that the offering of sacrifices could begin at once. Many priests and Levites were among those who returned. The feast of Tabernacles was the first festival to be held (Ezra 3¹⁻⁶).

Two years elapsed before the foundations of a new Temple were laid, and this was celebrated with much rejoicing although the elderly, who recalled the previous building, wept with emotion (Ezra 3⁶⁻¹³). Offers of help came from the Samaritans. They were the people who had taken the place of the old Northern Kingdom of Israel. They were descended from the Hebrews who had remained there, and from the new people brought in by Assyria. Their offer was refused because a new exclusive attitude had developed during the Exile. 'You have nothing to do with us in building a house to our God' was Zerubbabel's reply (Ezra 4³).

Because they were not allowed to help, the Samaritans set about hindering the work. Threats to the Jews and letters to the King of Persia caused work to stop for about sixteen years (Ezra 3–5).

Meanwhile people needed to rebuild their own homes. The land had been devastated and the work of reconstruction was a gigantic task. The first enthusiasm faded, but in 520 B.C. the prophet Haggai urged people to begin work again on the Temple. He said that the poor crops were the result of neglecting the Temple and building their own houses (Haggai 1–2). Zerubbabel started the work again, and, despite further attempts to stop it, was eventually supported by the decree of King Darius of Persia (Ezra 5–6).

Four years later, in 516 B.C., the Temple was dedicated, the returned priests were organized again into their twenty-four divisions, and all was ready to keep the next great festival, the Passover. Haggai had said, 'The latter splendour of this house shall be greater than the former, says the Lord of hosts; and in this place I will give prosperity' (Haggai 2⁹).

By comparison with Solomon's Temple, however, the rebuilt Temple was not elaborate, but the plan was similar. There were two courtyards, one leading to an inner one where the altar of burnt offering stood. The actual Temple building consisted of two chambers, the Holy Place with its altar of incense, table of Shewbread, and lampstand, leading to the Holy of Holies. Unlike Solomon's Temple, the Holy of Holies was empty, for the Ark of the Covenant was now lost.

The most difficult period in the Temple's history came with the persecution of the Jews by Antiochus Epiphanes IV, which began in 169 B.C. He entered the Temple, tore it to pieces, removed its golden altar and its treasures, and desecrated it still further by offering swine's flesh to Zeus upon the altar of burnt offering. No more Jewish sacrifices were allowed, for the worship of God was forbidden, the copies of the Law were burnt, and anyone who kept the Sabbath was to be put to death (1 Maccabees 1).

Judas Maccabaeus led the revolt against Antiochus Epiphanes. Once again a derelict Temple had to be repaired. It was now overgrown, and Judas chose priests to set about the task. A new altar of burnt offering was built and the one defiled by Antiochus was removed. New vessels were made, and on the 25th Chislev 164 B.C. a feast of Dedication was held (1 Maccabees 4³⁸⁻⁵⁹). It became an annual commemoration.

In 63 B.C. Pompey, the commander in chief of the Roman army, besieged Jerusalem. He broke into the Temple, and walked into the Holy of Holies. There was no resistance because it was the Sabbath, and thousands of Sadducees were massacred.

In 20 B.C. work began on the last and most magnificent of all the Temples. It was provided by Herod the Great.

On the 9th Ab, the fifth month of the Hebrew year, Jews observe a a fast to commemorate the destructions of their Temples.

Herod's Temple

Begun in 20 B.C. Herod's Temple took forty-six years to complete, and was still being built at the time of Jesus.

By comparison with the previous Temples, the new one was a magnificent affair of white marble with golden gates and domes. It was built on the top of Mount Moriah, the mountain said to have been the place of Abraham's projected sacrifice of Isaac. It also incorporated the site once occupied by Solomon's palace. Beneath the whole Temple area were numerous storerooms and stables.

As Herod's Temple was far more extensive than previous structures, the whole site had to be reconstructed.

The greater part of the Temple area, about 1000 feet square, was in the open air. Around the perimeter were colonnaded porticoes leading into an open courtyard known as the Court of the Gentiles, so named because Gentiles were permitted to enter only thus far. It was here that the money-changers were to be found, and those who sold animals for sacrifice.

The Court of the Gentiles was separated from the rectangular area of the inner courts by a 4½-foot marble wall, carrying warning notices in Greek and Latin that death was the penalty for any Gentile who went beyond. Inside the wall, a flight of fourteen steps and a terrace led upwards to the walls of the actual sanctuary.

This contained first another courtyard with rooms around it, and the thirteen money-boxes forming the Treasury. This was the Court of the

Women, so named because women were not allowed to pass on from that courtyard to the courts of the Levites and courts of the Priests. It was in the inner Court of the Priests that the altar of burnt offering stood.

Rising up in the midst of this court was the structure that formed the heart of the Temple. A porch, with two gold-plated doors covered by a rich curtain, led into the Holy Place, where stood the great golden seven-branched lampstand, the table of Shewbread and the altar of incense. Another door, covered by another curtain, led into a further chamber, the Holy of Holies or Most Holy Place. This was completely empty, save for a stone slab. It was entered but once a year, and then by the High Priest alone, on the Day of Atonement.

The Temple was the pride of all Jews. Many must have exclaimed, as did the disciples to Jesus: 'Look, Teacher, what wonderful stones and what wonderful buildings!' Jesus made the grim reply: 'Do you see these great buildings? There will not be left here one stone upon another, that will not be thrown down' (Mark 13[1,2]).

His words came true in A.D. 70 when the armies of Titus entered Jerusalem, and burned down the Temple on the feast of Pentecost. The arch of Titus in Rome commemorates the event. This put an end to sacrificial worship.

In 135 A.D. the city was again destroyed when Jewish rebels, under a semi-Messiah calling himself Bar-cochab ('son of a star'), were crushed by Roman forces. The Emperor Hadrian banned all Jews from the city, which he rebuilt, erecting therein a temple to Jupiter on the site of the Jewish Temple.

The site is now occupied by the Dome of the Rock (in allusion to Abraham), a Moslem mosque. A few stones of Herod's Temple remain. Jewish pilgrims visit this 'Wailing Wall', and there lament the lost glories of their Temple.

13. Sacrifice

The offering of sacrifice has been a world-wide feature in religious development. When people believed that their deities had moods and emotions similar to their own, it was thought that sacrifice was a means of putting a god into a beneficent mood, so that he would attend favourably to the requests of the worshipper. The actual smell of burning meat was thought to be pleasing to him.

Sometimes a sacrifice was a device for appeasing or placating a deity who was apparently angry. Drought and famine were obvious indications of divine displeasure.

Another form of sacrifice arose out of a desire to enter into communion with a deity, and share his vitality. This type of sacrifice was followed by a meal, of which the priests and worshippers partook. Part of the sacrifice was offered to the god, and the rest was eaten. In this way, by partaking of the same animal, deity and worshippers were brought into fellowship.

As late as the first century A.D. this form of sacrifice was common among Romans and Greeks. It presented a problem to the Christian Church, for many Gentile converts had but newly turned from this type of worship. The Christians at Corinth asked St. Paul whether they might eat meat left over from such sacrifices. There were also those who still wished to take part in pagan worship (1 Corinthians 10^{14-30}).

A further reason for sacrifice was a desire to give a present to a deity. It sometimes took the form of human sacrifice, not because human life was lightly regarded, but rather the reverse. Nothing but the costliest was thought good enough (see p. 88). This sort of gift sacrifice could also be a means of saying 'thank you'.

Examples of these types of sacrifice are to be found in the Old Testament. A fictional example from the story of Noah describes him, after leaving the ark, as building an altar and offering sacrifice. 'And when the Lord smelled the pleasing odour, the Lord said in his heart, "I will never again curse the ground. ... " ' (Genesis 8^{21}). This detail of the story is taken from the Babylonian original in the Epic of Gilgamesh, in which the gods gather round the sacrifice (Leviticus 23^{18}; Numbers $15^{3, 7, 10, 13, 24}$, $28^{6, 27}$).

The Hebrews came to realize that their God required more than such sacrifices. The prophets, such as Amos denouncing the sins of the Northern Kingdom, stressed the point that God could not be kept amiable merely by the offering of costly sacrifices. They would not distract his attention from social evils. Amos told the people of the north that social justice and righteousness was what God really required for he was weary of their sacrifices (Amos 5[21-24]). Isaiah expressed the same sentiments to the people of the south (Isaiah 1[11-17]), as also did Micah (Micah 6[7,8]).

The Hebrews eventually came to learn that they could not expect a sacrifice to appease their God. But in times of trouble they sometimes thought that it would, as we have seen in the case of the human sacrifice of seven descendants of King Saul (see p. 89).

After Jacob's vision, he took the stone upon which he had been resting his head, set it upright, and poured oil upon it. This was an offering to placate the spirit whom he felt must dwell within the stone which he had inadvertently chosen for a pillow (Genesis 28[11,18]).

The sacrificial meal was particularly frequent, because until the Deuteronomic Reform all the slaughter of domestic animals for food was sacrificial. The family went to the local high place, the animal was sacrificed, and the meat shared between priest and people, the blood representing the life having been poured out for God (1 Samuel 9[11-14], 19,[22-25]). These meals ended only when the Deuteronomic Reform closed down the high places, and permitted non-sacrificial slaughter of animals (Deuteronomy 12[15-16]).

Frequently in the law concerning festivals comes the command: 'None shall appear before me empty-handed' (Exodus 23[15], 34[20]; Deuteronomy 16[16]). This was a reminder to the worshipper always to bring some form of offering to God, especially at the great festivals of thanksgiving.

Not all offering involved the sacrifice of an animal. Cereals and wine were also presented. In the case of animal sacrifice the death of the animal was not the main purpose: it was the blood, representing the life, that was offered to God. Pouring out or sprinkling the blood, and burning the remains, or such part of the remains as was to be offered to God, was the only way of transforming them into a form in which God could receive them (Judges 6[21]). The death of the victim was, of course, inevitable, but incidental.

The Jewish sacrificial system became highly complex, especially after the Exile, when the priests reorganized much of the ceremonial law. Sacrifices can be classified in many ways, according to the offerings, the intentions, and the occasions, but the simplest classification is to divide them into private and public.

The private sacrifice was one offered by an individual or family for some private reason, e.g. purification after childbirth (Leviticus 12), vows, tithes, thanksgiving, sin, recovery from leprosy (Leviticus 14). These private sacrifices were further grouped into those prescribed and those voluntary.

Public sacrifices were those offered by the priests in the Temple on behalf of the nation, and on national occasions of thanksgiving or penitence. These consisted of daily sacrifices offered morning and evening, and the additional sacrifices for the Sabbath and the national festivals.

Oxen, sheep and goats were the sacrificial animals, and, in addition, turtle doves or young pigeons, which were usually an alternative offering for the poor. In private sacrifice the offerer himself killed the animal. In public sacrifices this was done by a priest acting as the people's representative.

An important feature of most private sacrifice was the laying on of the hands of the offerer or offerers. Hands were pressed hard upon the animal's head between the horns, and confession of sin was made before the animal was slain. The laying on of hands had a two-fold significance. First, it indicated that the animal was the offerer's very own possession: it was important that the worshipper offer to God something that really belonged to the offerer. Second, it indicated substitution, for the animal was being offered in place of the human being – another reason why it needed to be his own possession.

The confession of sin accompanying the laying on of hands was not intended to transmit guilt from the offerer to the victim, even in the case of a sin offering. The sacrifice was an offering *to* God. It included a request for forgiveness, but there was no question of the animal's death symbolizing a punishment *from* God on the sinner's substitute. The victim was not bearing the sins of the offerer, nor receiving the punishment due to him.

The only occasion when there was transmission of guilt was when the High Priest confessed the sins of the nation while, as the nation's representative, he laid his hands on the head of the 'scapegoat' on the Day of Atonement. This goat was not sacrificed (see p. 111). Sacrificial animals were sometimes eaten by priests and worshippers, and this would have been unthinkable if they acquired the offerers' sins. It was the sprinkling or throwing of the blood upon parts of the altar, before pouring the remainder away at its base, which made atonement (i.e. 'cover') for sin.

Thus a sacrifice was essentially a gift to God, made by an individual or a nation. It was accompanied by various petitions and thanksgivings, according to the motive of the offerer and the occasion of the offering.

The burnt offering

This type of sacrifice was particularly a gift offering. Apart from the skin, blood and the entrails, it was completely burned, and so given to God. It was an act of devotion by the individual or the nation. The daily morning and evening Temple sacrifices were burnt offerings, and as such were a continual token of Israel's allegiance to God. Additional burnt offerings marked the festivals (Exodus 29$^{38-42}$; Leviticus 1, 12$^{6-8}$; Deuteronomy 33^{10}; Psalm 51^{16,17}).

Even Gentiles could offer a burnt offering, and of these the most eminent and the most surprising was the first Roman Emperor, Augustus Caesar. He bought a daily burnt offering of two lambs and a bullock (Numbers 15$^{14-16}$).

The sin offering and the guilt offering

The sin offering, public or private, was intended to atone for the general sinfulness of the offerer. On festivals, sin offerings formed part of the observances, and national sinfulness was thus atoned for. Especially was this so on the Day of Atonement, when a bullock and a goat were the appointed sin offerings for that day.

Guilt offerings were private sacrifices for atonement for particular offences. Even so, sin in general or sin in particular had to be commited through ignorance, weakness or merely human nature, for any sacrifice to atone for it. Deliberate sin, committed 'with a high hand', had no means of atonement (Numbers 15^{30}).

During sin and guilt offerings the important feature was the sprinkling of the victim's blood, before the pouring of it at the foot of the altar. The sprinkling of the blood, particularly upon the corners or 'horns' of the altar, indicated that atonement had been made for the offerer.

Sometimes the flesh of the victim was eaten by the priests, sometimes it was burned, depending upon the precise type of sin or guilt offering (Leviticus 4-5, 8$^{14-17}$, 12$^{6-8}$, 14^{19}; Numbers 15$^{22-31}$; Psalm 19$^{12-13}$).

The peace offering

The important feature of this offering was the sacrificial meal partaken by priests and worshippers. This was the sacrifice that brought them into communion with God. The sacrifices were usually private, though there was a public peace offering as part of the celebrations of the feast of Pentecost, and at the consecration of priests.

Peace offerings always followed after other types of sacrifice, for they signified that the offerer had made his peace with God, and so could enter into fellowship with him. The particular intentions, other than free will, with which a worshipper might make a peace offering were thanksgiving and vows (Leviticus 3, $7^{11-18,28-36}$, 8^{22-32}, 9^4, 22^{21-23}, $23^{19,20}$; Numbers $6^{14,17-20}$; Deuteronomy 27^7; 1 Kings 8^{62-63}; Psalm 54^6, 56^{12}).

The meal offering

Besides the offerings of animals and birds as sacrifices, other products such as wine (drink offering), oil and cereals were used. All burnt offerings and peace offerings, whether public or private, were accompanied by a prescribed meal offering, but a meal offering could also be made on its own.

Notable among the public meal offerings were the twelve shewbread loaves presented each Sabbath, the first barley sheaf at the Passover, and the two newly-baked loaves 'waved' at Pentecost.

The offerings could be brought uncooked in the form of flour and oil, or specially cooked in the form of loaves, each consisting of not less than an *omer* of corn. The priest presented the meal offering on a golden dish. Then part of the offering was mixed with frankincense and burned. The remainder belonged to the priests. The wine (or drink offering), which always formed part of a meal offering, was poured out at the base of the altar (Exodus 25^{30}; Leviticus 2, 5^{11-13}, 7^{11-14}, 24^{5-9}; Numbers 5^{15-17}, $15^{9,10,19-21,24}$; 1 Samuel 21 $^{1-6}$).

The use in the Authorized Version of the term 'meat' where the Revised Standard Version uses 'meal' belongs to the time when 'meat' meant food in general and not, as now, flesh food in particular.

127

14. The Priesthood

Despite, or perhaps because of, the numerous references to priesthood in the Old Testament, the subject is one of the most perplexing, and no one has yet found a generally acceptable principle behind it. The majority of references come from the book of Leviticus, which forms the greater part of the exilic priestly source P, and from other passages from P.

During the Exile the priests had revised and reorganized much of the earlier forms of Hebrew worship. After the Exile their revised liturgies were put into practice. Consequently all references to the priesthood from the book of Leviticus and source P describe a very late stage in priestly organization. Furthermore, all the pre-exilic history recorded in the books of Samuel and Kings is presented by post-exilic editors for whom an organized priesthood was an established fact.

Before the Exile

Among ancient peoples the need for a priesthood was probably closely connected with the early idea of holiness as a contaminating force (see p. 90). Ordinary people had to keep away from anything holy. Some privileged people had to be appointed to do so on their behalf. They wore for the purpose protective clothing, washed off contamination with water, and sometimes removed shoes, so that contamination might not be carried to the rest of the community.

In early Hebrew times anyone could offer a sacrifice on behalf of himself or his tribe. Thus did Cain and Abel, and the patriarchs Noah, Abraham, Isaac and Jacob. The place could be almost anywhere, or at some recognized shrine (Genesis 8[20]J; 13[18]J, 15[9-17]J, 22[1-14]E, 26[25]J; Judges 6[25,26], 11[31]). Anyone so gifted could practise divination, as did Joseph (Genesis 44[5]). Furthermore, a tribal leader led his people both in war and in worship.

The question thus arises as to what was the function of an early Hebrew priest. Apparently he was the custodian of a shrine, the mouthpiece of the resident deity, and the minister for sacrificial purposes of anyone who wished to make use of him. Alternatively a priest was someone skilled in divination, and equipped with the necessary apparatus, who was employed by some eminent person as a sort of domestic chaplain, to act for him when he chose not to act for himself (Judges 17[5,7-13]; 1 Samuel 22[11-19], 30[7,8]).

Moses, as the founder of the Hebrew nation and the first leader of the people, was privileged to ascend the holy mountain, Sinai, when all others were forbidden to touch it (Exodus 19[3,12-14,20-24] J and E). The Covenant sacrifice was offered by him (Exodus 24[3-8]E).

It is not easy to tell from the Pentateuch whether Moses delegated any of his priestly duties to his older brother, Aaron. Moses did relieve himself of many civic duties and functions on the advice of his father-in-law, Jethro (Exodus 18[13-26]). Most of the mentions of Aaron and of his sons' being exalted to form a priesthood come from the late priestly writings (P). How far such writings record actual history, and how far they give back-dated origins of the post-exilic priestly elite, it is difficult to say. The early sources J and E mention only Aaron as accompanying Moses at his interviews with Pharaoh (Exodus 4[10-16,27-31], 5[1,4,20], 8[8-12] etc.).

Moses appointed Aaron, his sons, Nadab and Abihu, and seventy elders to positions of responsibility, but they were not priestly, although the men appointed were permitted to approach the holy mountain more closely (Exodus 24[1-14] J and E). This appointment was probably a direct result of Jethro's advice.

The only early record of any priestly action by Aaron is that of his making a golden calf for people to worship (Exodus 32[1-24]E), and of Moses and Aaron's own tribe of Levi rallying to Moses' cry 'Who is on the Lord's side?', and proceeding to purge the community of the idolatrous worshippers (Exodus 32 [25-34]J). It must be remembered that the condemnation of Aaron's action may be due to later religious ideas (see p. 9).

The early priesthood was not exclusive to the tribe of Levi. It appears that priesthood was a vocation for anyone who wanted to specialize in some sort of priestly work. Even the term Levite could be used for someone of a different tribe (Judges 17[7]). Source J mentions Joshua, who was not a Levite, as being the first appointed guardian of the Tabernacle (Exodus 33[6-11]). Eli and Samuel, the custodians of the Ark of the Covenant in the sanctuary at Shiloh, were also non-Levites (1 Samuel 1[1,3,9]). Micah's hired priest was a 'Levite' of the tribe of Judah (Judges 17[7-13]). This seems to indicate that the terms 'priest' and 'Levite' were alternative terms (as in Deuteronomy). It was not until later that the terms indicated difference in status.

After the Ark of the Covenant was returned by the Philistines it remained in the house of Abinadab, 'and they consecrated his son Eleazar, to have charge of the ark of the Lord' (1 Samuel 7[1]). Before the

Ark's eventual arrival in Jerusalem it stayed for three months in the house of Obed-edom, the Gittite (2 Samuel 6[11]). Elijah, a non-Levite, the great prophet of the Northern Kingdom, offered sacrifice at Mount Carmel (1 Kings 18).

The Hebrew king, as well as being the political leader, was the representative of his people before God. His anointing was a sign of the priestly side of his work (see p. 44). Thus the king led his people in worship, and on special occasions offered sacrifice. Samuel was not prepared to recognize this function of a king when Saul offered sacrifice on behalf of his army before battle (1 Samuel 13[8-13]), and Saul does not appear to have claimed it in excuse for his action.

David, dressed as a priest, offered sacrifices when the Ark of the Covenant was brought to Jerusalem (2 Samuel 6[13,14,17-19]). Solomon presided at the services of dedication of his Temple (1 Kings 8). Jeroboam I of the Northern Kingdom himself offered sacrifices at the shrines of Dan and Bethel (1 Kings 12[32,33]). The Hebrew kings did not belong to the tribe of Levi.

Organized priesthood, it seems almost certain, began with King David. He brought the Ark to Jerusalem, and placed it in a tent (2 Samuel 6[17]). He had plans to build for it a more permanent house (2 Samuel 7[2,3], verses 4–13 being later comment by Deuteronomic editors). King David also is said to have organized the priests into twenty-four divisions, but priestly traditions tried to trace this back to Moses and Aaron (1 Chronicles 24).

Much palace intrigue surrounded Solomon's accession to the throne. Abiathar the priest supported the claims to the throne of Adonijah, David's oldest surviving son, but Zadok the priest was a supporter of Solomon, a much younger son. When Solomon was proclaimed king by his dying father, it was Zadok who anointed him (1 Kings 1). Abiathar was expelled by Solomon to his home in Anathoth (1 Kings 2[26,27]). Zadok and his family were promoted (1 Kings 4[1-4]).

Thus with Zadok and his family, said to be descended from Aaron (1 Chronicles 6[1-8]), there was formed a select priestly hierarchy in charge of the new Temple. Azariah, the grandson of Zadok, was appointed 'the priest'. So the presiding Zadokite became known as *the* priest, or the 'great' or 'high' priest, to distinguish him from all the lesser priestly officials (2 Kings 22[4], 23[4]).

From the entry into Canaan until the Deuteronomic Reform of 621 B.C. sacrifices could be offered to God at any of the recognized sanctuaries, and at the local high places also used for Baal worship. All these places needed a Yahweh priesthood, whether they were in the Northern Kingdom of Israel or in the Southern Kingdom of Judah. Thus Eli, his sons, and Samuel were priests at Shiloh; Samuel officiated at Ramah;

Ahimelech and his family were priests at Nob; Jeroboam, the first king of the Northern Kingdom, was later condemned for appointing a non-levitical priesthood to the northern shrines of Dan and Bethel (1 Kings 12[31,32]).

The Deuteronomic Reform prohibited the use of high places for sacrifices to Yahweh. In future the Temple only would be the place for sacrificial worship. Consequently all the priests who served the high places were unemployed. They were allowed to come to Jerusalem to serve the Temple, and to share in the Temple income, together with the ordinary Jerusalem priests (Deuteronomy 18[6–8]). This was probably the beginning of the subordinate order of Levites as distinct from the priests.

Up to the time of the Exile, therefore, there was no distinction between the significance of the terms 'priest' or 'Levite'. The majority of the priests were indeed members of the tribe of Levi, though the priestly vocation was not exclusive to that tribe. Certainly the tribe of Levi had acquired the monopoly of the priesthood (Deuteronomy 18[1–5]) and within that tribe the Zadokites formed a Temple hierarchy.

During the Exile

Sacrificial worship was not possible during the Exile, for the recent Deuteronomic Reform had restricted this to Jerusalem. The priests re-edited their history, and made plans for the future. Ezekiel the priest planned the ideal Temple of the future with its ideal priesthood (Ezekiel 40–46). He also helped to raise the hopes of his people that one day God would let the nation live again.

A new non-sacrificial type of worship was devised during the Exile. It consisted of readings from the Law and the writings of the Prophets, the singing of psalms, and exhortations by the Scribes, who were those who made copies of the Law and so became its experts. This was the beginning of the synagogue worship of later years.

The synagogues became the local places in which Jews could worship. They did not require priests, and so the services and their upkeep were in the hands of 'rulers'. Any group of worthy Jews could form a committee of rulers of a synagogue. The services were conducted by a Rabbi. The word Rabbi originated in Babylonia. In various forms it signified degree of rank, e.g. head steward of a household, principal adviser to a ruler, commander in chief of an army. Among the Jews in New Testament times the word was the equivalent of Master or Teacher (Matthew 23[7,8]; Luke 11[45]; John 1[38, 49]). It is now the usual title of a senior member of the Jewish clergy.

After the Exile

After the Exile, under the influence of Ezekiel (Ezekiel 44[9-16]), two grades of Temple ministrants emerged, and a third became distinct – Levites, priests, and Zadokites.

Anyone who was of the tribe of Levi could serve the Temple as a Levite. The Levites were the Temple servants, responsible for keeping it clean, attending to its stores, acting as sacristans, guarding its gates, acting as Temple police. During service they acted as choristers and priests' assistants.

The priesthood was available to suitable claimants of descent from Aaron. The Aaronic priesthood comprised the many hundreds of priests, in their twenty-four divisions, responsible for all the daily worship in the Temple throughout the year. Many lived in Jerusalem, or in nearby towns such as Anathoth and Jutha, though some lived further afield. Each division was on duty for two weeks in the year, and all priests in that division had to attend the Temple during its time of duty. All divisions were on duty at the feast of Tabernacles.

Evidently there was some resentment against the distinction between Levites and priests, or the priestly writers anticipated it, for they included in the Pentateuch a cautionary story about a deputation to Moses. The reasons for it are confused because of much re-editing. Firstly, Korah and his supporters are laymen protesting at the privileges given to Levites (Numbers 16[3]). Secondly, he and his supporters are Levites demanding the status of priests (Numbers 16[10]). In point of fact the distinction was post-exilic. The rebels were swallowed up and burned with fire (Numbers 16[32, 35]).

The priestly writers mixed their story with an earlier one of a rebellion against Moses by Dathan and Abiram (sources J and E; cf. Deuteronomy 11[6]).

The Zadokites, later the Sadducees, formed the select ruling priestly party. The Zadokite priests were the chief priests. They lived in Jerusalem and controlled the Temple. The High Priest was always a Zadokite. He of all the priests represented the people and was head of the community. He had an official house in the Temple, in addition to his own private dwelling.

When not officiating at the Temple, priests did not wear distinctive clothing.

Since the office of High Priest had first come into being with the appointment of Zadok's grandson, the position was hereditary and held for life. Unfortunately in the Greek period appointment to the High Priesthood became corrupted by political intrigue. The office could be bought for money.

After the Exile the Hebrew monarchy was not re-established, and thus the High Priest was anointed, and took the place of the king, until in 37 B.C. the ambitious Herod, with Roman support, claimed the throne. Even then the High Priest was exceedingly powerful. After Herod's death in 4 B.C. the kingdom was divided among his sons, and so again the High Priest was the one who held overall authority, even, on occasion, making the Roman Governor bow to his wishes.

Index

Aaron, 9, 35, 40, 76, 78, 105, 118, 129–30, 132
Abiathar, 130
Abihu, 129
Abinadab, 36, 91–2, 119, 129
Abiram, 132
Abraham, 5, 15, 19, 26, 29, 31, 38–40, 49, 58, 61–2, 67–8, 70, 82–6, 88, 93, 99, 114–15, 121–2, 128
Achan, 21, 91
Adam and Eve, 13, 63–4
Adonijah, 27, 130
Adonis, 83
After-life, 24, 73, 96–102
Ahab, 22, 36–7, 43–5, 78
Ahaz, 45, 48, 98–9
Ahimelech, 131
Ai, 21, 91
Alexandria, 53, 57
Amalekites, 17, 21, 87
Amorites, 29, 78
Amos, 10, 16, 22–3, 28, 37, 47, 50–51, 54, 58, 70, 99, 124
Anathoth, 130, 132
Animism, 81
Annas, 45
Antiochus Epiphanes, 113, 120–21
Aphrodite, 83
Apocalypse, 59–60
Apocrypha, 53–7, 102
Aramean, 29
Ark of the Covenant, 9, 13, 22, 32, 35–6, 45, 80, 85, 87, 91–2, 109, 111, 118–20, 129, 130
Asherah, 93–4
Ashtoreth (*pl.* Ashtaroth), 51, 81, 93–5
Assyrians, 37, 42–3, 71, 88–9
Astarte, 83, 92
Atonement, Day of, 110, 113, 122, 125–6
Authors and editors of O.T., 4–9, 12–14, 52, 61, 75, 100
Azariah, 130

Baal, 6, 10, 17, 21–4, 36–7, 43, 52, 81, 85–6, 88, 93–5, 130
Babel, 61, 65–6
Babylon, Babylonian, 32, 35, 38, 42, 58, 62–3, 65–8, 70–2, 74, 82–3, 86, 88–9, 92, 95–6, 98, 101, 104, 116, 119, 123
Bar-cochab, 122
Bathsheba, 44
Bethel, 7, 8, 10, 19, 22, 33, 43, 82–3, 87, 130–31
Bethlehem, 48, 69, 99
Beth-shemesh, 80, 87
Book of the Dead, 33, 96
Bronze serpent, 79
Burning bush, 20, 83, 86, 91
Burnt offering, 126

Caiaphas, 45
Cain and Abel, 64, 128
Canaan, Canaanite, 5, 20, 21, 29–30, 35, 39, 40–42, 75, 77, 92–3, 95, 118, 130
Carmel, Mt., 36, 77, 86, 130
Ceres, 83, 92
Chemosh, 21, 25, 93
Chosen People, 5, 18–19, 24, 38, 47, 61, 68–70
Circumcision, 4, 24
Covenant, 1, 12, 14, 18, 20, 28–38, 68, 85, 88–9, 93, 104, 107–8, 129
Creation, 12–13, 33, 56, 61–5
Cybele, 83
Cyrus, 47, 119

Dan, 7–8, 10, 22, 33, 40, 43, 83, 130–31
Daniel, 54, 60
Dathan, 132
David, 22, 30, 36, 41–6, 48–9, 58, 68, 83, 89, 92, 119, 130
Day of the Lord, 58
Deborah, 41, 82–3, 99
Decalogue (Ten Commandments), 9, 14, 28, 30–34,

50, 62, 85, 104, 107 108, 115–16
Dedication, feast of, 113, 121
Demeter, 83, 92
Deuteronomic Reform, 4, 6–8, 10–11, 43, 49–50, 54, 100, 105, 115, 124, 130–31
Deuteronomy, 4, 7–8, 10, 14, 33, 50, 54, 89, 93, 95, 105, 107, 115, 124, 129
Divination, 128

Egypt, Egyptian, 4–5, 28–31, 33, 39–41, 48, 58, 61, 71, 76, 85, 88, 98, 104–5, 115
El, Elohim, El-Shaddai, 13, 19, 25, 27, 84, 87
Eleazar, 36, 92, 130
Eli, 35, 94, 129–30
Elijah, 10, 17, 22, 27, 36, 44–5, 77–8, 80, 85–6, 94, 130
Elisha, 36, 78
Esther, 53–4, 70–71, 73, 114
Euphrates, 39, 67
Exile, 4, 8, 14, 17, 22–4, 38, 42, 49, 51–2, 55, 62, 68, 71, 92, 95, 98, 100–101, 104, 110, 113, 116, 118, 120, 128, 130
Exodus, book of, 4, 14, 33, 50, 54, 76, 106, 116
Exodus, the, 4, 17–19, 28, 30, 40–41, 48, 61, 71, 76, 85, 104–105, 116
Ezekiel, 8, 50, 54, 57, 89, 131–2
Ezra, 51, 54, 68

Fall, the, 61, 63–4, 68
Fertile crescent, 19, 29, 35, 39
Fertility cults, 81, 83, 92–5
Festivals, 104

Genesis, book of, 14, 19, 39, 49, 50, 54, 56, 61, 67, 76

134

Gentiles, 24, 38, 55, 68, 69–70, 72, 116, 121, 123, 126
Gibeonites, 30, 89
Gideon, 83, 85, 93
Gilgal, 79, 87
Gilgamesh, 67, 123
Gnostic sects, 65
God, ideas of, 15–25, 51, 55–7, 68, 73, 75, 90–91, 95, 98, 100–101, 116, 119
name of, 25–7
Golden calf, 8–9, 31, 33, 129
Guilt offering, 126

Habakkuk, 54
Hagar, 13, 40, 84
Haggai, 51, 54, 104, 120
Hallel, 106, 109, 114
Haman, 71–2, 114
Hammurabi, 31, 33, 34, 39, 115
Haran, 19, 39–40, 115
Herod, 49, 121, 133
Hezekiah, 43, 45, 47, 79, 94, 101
High places, 23, 86, 93–5, 124, 130–31
High Priest, 45–6, 97, 110–12, 118, 125, 130, 132–3
Hittite, 29–30
Holiness, 14, 23, 89–92, 128
Holy of Holies, 110–12, 119–22
Horeb, Mt., 20, 28, 31, 83, 85
Hosea, 10, 23, 37, 48, 51, 54, 115
Hyksos, 39–40

Images, 9, 82
Isaac, 13, 19, 29, 40, 61, 85–6, 88, 93, 121, 128
Isaiah, 23, 37, 45, 47–8, 50–51, 54, 58, 70, 90, 98, 115
Isaiah, Deutero-, 17, 51, 56, 62
Ishmael, 13, 40, 84
Ishtar, 71, 83, 92, 96
Isis, 83
Israel, 6, 24, 28–9, 36–7, 42, 45–6, 58, 70, 73, 83, 85, 89, 93–4, 99–100, 118, 126

Jacob, 19, 29, 39–40, 61, 82, 85–7, 98, 124, 128
Jamnia, 2, 53
Jashar, 78
Jehoiakim, 45
Jehovah, 26
Jeremiah, 8, 10, 37, 45, 47–8, 50, 54–6, 89, 94
Jericho, 3–4, 21, 77, 79, 91
Jeroboam, 1, 8–11, 83, 130–31
Jerusalem, 10, 22, 36, 41, 45, 59, 69, 89, 92, 94–5, 98, 108, 119, 121, 130–32
Jeshua, 120
Jesus, 1, 24, 32, 38, 47–8, 59, 64, 70, 72–4, 97, 107, 116, 121–2
Jethro (Moses' father-in-law), 18, 27, 30, 34, 76, 129
Jezebel, 10, 22, 36–7, 43–4, 77, 99
Job, 53–4, 72–4, 98, 101–102
Joel, 51, 54
John the Baptist, 47, 58
Jonah, 24, 54, 69–71, 73
Jordan, 77, 79, 87
Joseph, 13–14, 29, 40, 54, 98
Joshua, 15, 30, 40–42, 77–9, 87, 89, 91, 128
Josiah, 7–8, 23, 43, 89, 94–5, 100, 105
Judah, 6, 9, 30, 41–3, 46, 83–4, 91, 94, 129
Judas Maccabaeus, 113, 121
Judges, 21, 35, 42, 68, 99

Kingship, 44–6, 130
Korah, 132

Laban, 40, 87
Law, the, 8, 24, 34, 49–50, 52–3, 90, 95, 99, 131
Leah, 40
Levi, 14, 40, 129, 131–2
Levirate marriage, 68, 99
Levites, 120, 122, 129, 131–2
Leviticus, book of, 13–14, 50, 54, 110, 118, 128
Lights, feast of, 113–14
Logos, 57
Lot, 40, 79
Lots, feast of, 71–2

Luke, 58

Maccabees, Maccabaean, 45, 102
Malachi, 51, 54
Manasseh, 7, 89
Marcionite, 18
Marduk, 62, 71
Matthew, 47–8, 59
Meal offering, 127
Megillah, 114
Melchizedek, 45
Melkart, 10, 21–2, 25, 36–7, 44, 77, 86, 93–4
Messiah, 24, 41, 47–8, 52, 58–9, 74, 101, 107
Micah, 48, 51, 54, 124
Milcom, 21, 25, 93
Miracles, 75–80
Mizpah, 87
Moab, Moabites, 68, 86, 89, 93, 99
Molech, 21, 25, 89, 93
Moon worship, 39, 112, 114–15
Mordecai, 71–2, 114
Moses, 3, 5, 8–9, 18–21, 23, 26–8, 30–34, 40, 42, 49–50, 56, 61–2, 76, 78–9, 83, 85–6, 90–91, 105, 109–10, 118, 129–30, 132
Mountain spirits, 82, 85–6

Naboth, 44
Nadab, 129
Nathan, 44–5
Nationalism, 17
Nehemiah, 51, 54
New Year's Day, 112
Noah, 14, 40, 67–8, 123, 128
Nomads, 39
Northern Kingdom, 6–8, 10, 22, 33, 36, 41–3, 46, 58, 89, 115, 120, 124, 130–31
Numbers, book of, 14, 50, 54, 84, 118

Obed-edom, 36, 92, 119, 130
Omri, 43
Osiris, 33, 83, 96

Parables, 59, 61–8
Passover, feast of, 4, 71, 88, 104–107, 112, 120, 127

INDEX

Patriarchs, 19, 26, 72
Paul, 1, 15, 64, 97, 123
Peace offering, 126
Pentateuch, 8, 12–14, 49–50, 76, 104, 114, 118, 129, 132
Pentecost, feast of, 66, 104, 107–108, 122, 126–7
Persephone, 83
Pharaoh, 4, 40, 76, 78, 96, 105, 129
Pharisees, 24, 32, 38, 46, 97, 107
Philistines, 4, 35, 41–2, 78, 80, 83, 87, 91, 119
Pompey, 121
Priesthood, 90, 128–32
Priestly writers, 4, 13, 21, 62, 104, 115, 118, 131–2
Prophecy, 47–8, 52
Prophets, 16, 36–8, 48, 51–2, 58, 70, 82
Prophets, the, 24, 49–54, 95, 131
Proserpina, 83
Psalms, 45, 53–4, 56, 95, 103, 106, 109, 114, 131
Purim, feast of, 71–2, 114

Rabbi, 131
Rachel, 40, 87, 89
Ramah, 83, 93, 99, 130
Rebekah, 40, 82, 99
Red Sea, 76–7, 86
Rehoboam, 41, 46
Ruth, 24, 30, 54, 68–9, 99

Sabbath, 4, 33–4, 62, 109, 113–16, 121, 125, 127
Sacrifice, 23, 28, 45, 87–9, 93, 95, 104–106, 108, 110–13, 120, 123–31
Sadducees, 25, 45, 50, 97, 121, 132
Samaritans, 120
Samson, 4, 78
Samuel, 17, 21, 42, 45, 54, 87, 93, 100, 129–30
Saul, 41–2, 45, 54, 83, 87, 89, 93, 99–100, 124, 130
Scapegoat, 111, 125
Scribes, 24, 32, 116, 131
Semitic, 40, 41
Septuagint, 53
Servant Songs, 24, 56, 69, 73–4, 101
Shamash, 31
Shechinah, 55–6, 109
Sheol, 98, 101, 113
Sheshbazzar, 119
Shewbread, 120, 122, 127
Shiloh, 35, 130
Shurpu, 33
Sin offering, 126
Sinai, Mt., 18, 20, 28–32, 35, 50, 76, 85–6, 90, 93, 104, 107, 129
Solomon, 8–10, 22, 26, 34, 36, 41, 44–6, 54–5, 87, 109, 111, 119–21, 130
Sources, 12–14, 32
Southern Kingdom, 6–8, 13, 41, 46, 58, 130
Spirit of God, 55–7, 109
Sumerian, 67
Synagogue worship, 24, 95, 108, 114, 131

Tabernacle, the, 4, 56, 110, 118, 129
Tabernacles, feast of, 104, 108–110, 113, 120, 132
Tammuz, 82–3
Temple, the, 4, 7–10, 22–3, 38, 45, 62, 69, 79, 87–9, 94–5, 104, 107–109, 111, 113–14, 118–22, 125, 130–32
Terah, 39
Testament, 1
Tiamat, 62
Tigris, 39, 67
Titus, 122
Tree spirits, 81–3
Trumpets, feast of, 112–13

Unleavened Bread, feast of 104–107
Ur, 19, 39, 115
Uriah, 30
Uzzah, 36, 91–2

Vulgate, 53

Water spirits, 81, 83–4
Wisdom, 25, 54–5, 57–8
Wisdom Literature, 54, 102
Word of God, 55–7
Writing, 2, 32
Writings, the, 49, 52–3

Yahweh, 9–11, 13, 18, 20–29, 31, 33, 35–6, 43, 46, 51–2, 62, 68, 76, 78, 81, 85, 88–90, 94, 100, 105, 108, 115, 131

Zadok, 45, 130
Zadokites, 45, 130–32
Zechariah, 48, 51, 54
Zephaniah, 54
Zerubbabel, 47, 119–20
Ziggurats, 65